the
WiTCH's
journal

the W.I.T.C.H'S journal

charms, spells, potions and enchantments

SELENE SILVERWIND

A QUARTO BOOK

First published in the UK in 2009 by
Apple Press
74-77 White Lion Street
London N1 9PF
UK

www.apple-press.com
Reprinted in 2011, 2012, 2013
Copyright © 2009
Quarto Publishing plc

ISBN: 978-1-84543-309-3

Conceived, designed and produced by
Quarto Publishing plc
The Old Brewery
6 Blundell Street
London N7 9BH

QUA: BWM

Editor & designer: Michelle Pickering
Proofreader: Julia Halford
Indexer: Dorothy Frame
Art director: Caroline Guest
Design assistant: Saffron Stocker

Creative director: Moira Clinch
Publisher: Paul Carslake

Colour separation by Modern Age
Repro House Ltd, Hong Kong
Printed by Toppan Leefung
Printing Ltd, China

NOTE: The author, publisher and
copyright holder have made every
reasonable effort to ensure that the
recipes and rituals in this book are
safe when used as instructed, but
assume no responsibility for any
injury or damage caused or sustained
while using them.

Contents

Magical and Divinatory Tools 54

Spells, Charms and Potions 96

INTRODUCTION

Every Witch spends her life gathering little bits of knowledge, spells, charms, potions and lore. Traditionally, this information is kept in a Book of Shadows, or in the modern age, a Disk of Shadows. This book is a version of a Book of Shadows, but one designed for someone unfamiliar with the ways of Witchcraft.

Embarking on a Magical Path

Although Wicca – the religion associated with Witchcraft – began with a strict training hierarchy, most Witches are now self-taught.

Your Book of Shadows holds all your magical knowledge.

- There is no need to be initiated or trained by an elder; instead, you can create your own system based on your beliefs, knowledge and experience.
- Your intuition is the most important magical tool that you possess. Follow it, and it will guide you well on your magical path.
- Witchcraft does not require any special skills, talents or supernatural powers. It is actually based on the most natural thing in the world: your energy and will, as well as the energy of every other thing on the planet and in the heavens.
- If you have faith in your ability to use magic, you will succeed as a Witch.

Initiated Wiccans wear a cord around the waist during rituals.

Learning the Basics

This book provides all of the basic knowledge that you need in order to incorporate magic into your daily life.

- Magic begins with ethics. Follow the simple guidelines on pages 12–13 and you can be assured that you will stay on the right path.
- The basic building blocks of magic are explained in Chapter 1. These start with the magical correspondences of colours, stones and crystals, herbs, the planets and the moon.
- Witches worship many gods and goddesses from a variety of ancient pantheons. Chapter 1 includes an introduction to several pantheons popular among Witches, some of which are not well known to the general public.
- Chapter 2 explains the history and use of the most common magical tools, from the wand to the cauldron.
- In addition to physical tools, Witches also rely on divination to guide them in magic and in life. The most common divination methods are introduced in Chapter 2, with basic instructions on using them.

Sage is a powerful magical herb.

Witches use runes for divination.

Spells and Potions

- Once you have learned the basics, you are ready to try casting the spells and making the potions in Chapter 3.
- When a specific oil, herb, ingredient or tool is called for, you may substitute something else from the same family or with the same magical associations. Refer to Chapters 1 and 2 for ideas.

- If you are not comfortable calling upon a specific deity, you can substitute a different one with similar associations. For example, you could substitute Isis in place of Aphrodite during a love spell. You could also simply call upon the goddess or god as an archetype, any higher power, even the universe – whatever you feel comfortable with.

Writing Your Own Spells
If you are new to magic, it is best to cast a spell as it is written the first time. After that, use the basic spell outline to create your own. The one you write yourself will be far more powerful than any spell you find in a book, but only if you understand the basics and have faith in your abilities as a Witch.

A Final Caveat

Despite your best intentions, sometimes spells do not turn out as planned.

- You have to be careful not to leave the door too wide open when crafting spells. The gods operate on a different time frame than we do, so specify how soon you wish to receive the result. Be reasonable in your request – most spells cannot be granted overnight.

- You may also find that a spell does not work at all. When a spell fails, it is usually because the gods determined that it was not the best course of action for you. Or, they may allow a spell to succeed, only for you to realize that you should not have performed it in the first place. Consider it a lesson learned and then move on with your life and your magical practice. As long as you intend to do no harm, no spell can go too horribly awry.

Different Traditions

As you continue on your magical practice, you will discover many bits of lore or knowledge that are not contained in this book. You will also find different words and rituals used in different books and traditions, although their essence usually remains the same. There is a saying: 'If you ask 12 Witches a question, you will get 13 answers.' It means that there is not one exact way of doing anything in Witchcraft.

If you follow your heart, your intuition and your common sense, your magical journey will go smoothly and be richly rewarding. Just remember always to keep a sense of humour about your spells – the gods certainly do.

Blessed be

Selene Silverwind

How to Use This Book

This book is not meant to be read in order from first to last page, although you can if you wish. Think of it as a reference book. When a love spell mentions a specific oil or goddess, for example, flip to the relevant section for more information about why it is included. Use the magical symbols to guide you.

Magical Symbols

You will find a column of magical symbols at the edge of the left-hand pages in Chapters 1, 2 and 3. These serve two purposes. Firstly, they will help you to identify which section you are in as you flip back and forth through the book looking for information. Secondly, many of these symbols are traditional magical symbols that can be worn to represent your faith or incorporated into your spellwork. For example, draw the pentacle on parchment to enhance the energy of a spell.

△ Colours

☆ Heavenly bodies

✛ Divinatory tools

⊕ Stones and crystals

☥ Gods and goddesses

⛤ Spells and charms

⚡ Herbs

⋃ Magical tools

☘ Potions

WHAT IS MAGIC?

Magic is both a science and an art. It is a science in the sense that performing a spell requires research and an awareness of the methods of Witchcraft. It is an art in the sense that you need to follow your intuition and be creative. When practising magic, you blend the two to bend the natural forces to your will and bring about your desired outcome.

Black Magic vs White Magic

Black magic is simply magic that is intended to harm another being, or manipulate their free will. White magic is intended to bring about a positive outcome. However, there is some grey area. Casting a love spell to make someone you love return your feelings may seem positive, but because it involves manipulating the other person's free will, it is black magic. Some people reserve the term black magic for acts that draw on evil forces, but Wiccan Witches are more conservative in their views of black magic.

Types of Magic

There are several types of magic, but the four most common are:

- **Folk magic** includes old superstitions and folk practices, and continues to have power today, such as burying a statue of St Joseph upside down in the garden to speed the sale of a house.

- **Natural magic** is the use of herbs, stones and candles to direct energy. Natural magic also incorporates the moon, sun and planets.

- **Ceremonial magic** entails performing rituals, using specific props and speaking elaborate words; it is often called High Magic.

- **Sympathetic magic** is the use of objects that represent your desired outcome; for example, turning on the shower to make it rain.

There are many folk superstitions about black cats because of their association with Witches.

Witch or Wiccan?

Although you will hear the terms used interchangeably, Witch and Wiccan actually mean two different things.

- **A Witch** uses magic, also known as Witchcraft, to manipulate the energy of the universe to achieve a desired goal. Anyone of any religion can be a Witch.

- **A Wiccan** follows the religion called Wicca, a Neo-pagan religion based on re-creations of pre-Christian beliefs and practices, the worship of the earth and traditions adopted from ceremonial magic. Although Wiccans call themselves Witches, using Witchcraft is not a requirement. Many choose to use magic, while others simply honour the cycle of the seasons, the moon and the gods without using magic to achieve personal goals.

- **Pagans**, also known as Neo-pagans, follow one of several earth religions that are influenced by ancient Pagan religions. Wicca is one such earth religion. Druidry and Asatru (Norse) are the other two most common earth religions.

Other Terms for Magic
You might run across other terms for magic, including magick and the Craft, in other books. Wicca is sometimes referred to as the Old Religion.

Witch's Pyramid

Many Witches follow the rule known as the Witch's Pyramid. At its base are four actions, and at the top is the goal.

The Goal: The desired goal will only be obtained when all four actions at the base of the pyramid are carried out.

To Keep Silent: Once you have completed the spell, do not discuss it with others or think about it. Later mental energy could corrupt the original energy and weaken the spell.

To Dare: Have the courage to seek your goal and the willingness to accept the consequences.

To Will: Be strong in your desire to achieve your goal, and confident that you can do it.

To Know: Be clear in your objective.

THE ETHICS OF WITCHCRAFT

To ensure that you are firmly on the path of white Witchcraft, you should abide by the following ethics. Although not all Witches follow all of these suggestions, the spells in this book do. Not only will practising ethical magic prevent you from violating anyone else, but you will also protect yourself from a nasty magical backlash.

Four Rules for Magic
Always weigh the motivation and possible consequences of your spells carefully. Abide by these four rules to avoid casting unethical spells.

1 Do not cast a spell on another person without their permission.
2 Do not cast a spell to harm yourself or another person.
3 Do not cast a spell in haste.
4 Do not cast a spell in anger.

Wiccan Rede

The Wiccan Rede first appeared as a 26-line poem in *Earth Religion News* in 1974. It is usually summarized by the last line:

'An' it harm none, do what thou wilt.'

This means that you can do whatever you want as long as it harms no one. The tricky part is that 'no one' includes you. Avoid casting spells that will harm yourself. Harm is also considered to be anything that manipulates another person's free will. So, if you cast a spell to protect a friend from getting a broken heart, you could actually be causing harm by preventing the end of an unhealthy relationship.

The Golden Rule

The Wiccan Rede is similar to the Golden Rule found in many cultures: treat others as you would like them to treat you.

The Law of Three

- The Law of Three, which is primarily followed by Wiccan Witches, states that anything you put out will return to you threefold. So, if you are generally a positive person, positive things will happen in your life.
- Unfortunately, the threefold law can take a nasty turn if you cast a manipulative spell. For example, if you cast a spell to make a specific person fall in love with you, your love for him or her will be three times stronger, and could become an obsession.
- Think of the Law of Three as a version of karma — everything you do has an impact on your future self, for good or ill.

Try using divination to assess whether casting a spell is the right course of action.

Questions to Ask Before Casting a Spell

In addition to remembering the four rules, the Wiccan Rede and the Law of Three, you should ask yourself the following four questions before performing any spell to make sure that it is the right course of action.

1 **What are all the possible outcomes of this spell (positive and negative)?**

2 **Am I manipulating anyone else's free will?**

3 **Would I be willing to cause the outcome without a spell?**

4 **Is there an easier way to do this?**

Healing Spells

As with any rules, there are exceptions. You can cast a healing spell on another person without their permission if they are not able to give it. If the person is unconscious or a child, include a statement in the spell allowing the person's higher spirit to reject the healing energy as it sees fit.

Quickie spells

You can cast a spell in haste for quick things like getting a parking space or protecting yourself from imminent danger or harm. The haste rule applies to emotionally charged situations when you may not be thinking clearly.

CHAPTER ONE

Magical Correspondences

The subjects covered in this chapter are the building blocks of any spell. Although you do not have to incorporate every element into every spell, it is important to be familiar with them so that you can construct the best spell for your purpose. The basics include the magical associations of colours, stones and crystals, herbs, the planets and the moon, as well as the many ancient deities that you can call upon for assistance.

COLOURS

Colour is one of the most powerful magical energies available. Different colours are associated with certain concepts and aspects of life – for example, red for passion, green for growth and blue for communication. Fortunately, it is easy to incorporate colour into your rituals. Magic uses the most basic colours – no fuchsia or puce here. Instead, you draw on the colours in a crayon box: red, pink, orange, yellow, green, blue, purple, gold, silver, brown, black and white.

Colour Associations
Each colour is associated with a specific energy, planet and day of the week (see pages 102–103). When choosing the best colour for a spell, study all of the colour's associations and pick the colour or colours most appropriate to your primary goal. You can use intertwined ribbons or a multicoloured candle to fuse the energy of several colours together.

Incorporating Colour into Spells

Colour is a part of every aspect of life, so it is very easy to incorporate into your spells. To include colour energy in your magic, all you need is an object in the desired colour. You can wear or carry the object after the spell is complete to enhance its continued effect. The easiest ways to incorporate colour are:

- Altar cloths
- Ink pens, crayons and pencils
- Stones and crystals
- Unscented candles
- Robes or other clothing
- Ribbons and thread
- Painted objects

Chakra Colours

In yoga philosophy, there are seven main centres of physical or spiritual energy in the human body. These centres are called chakras. The colours of the visible spectrum are very important to the chakras and chakra healing. If you are performing a spell that requires healing or opening one of the chakras, or the part of the body that it rules, use the appropriate colour in your spell.

Chakra Healing

Lay an object, such as a natural stone, in the appropriate colour on a chakra point to help open it up. To rebalance your entire system, lie on your back and place one stone on each chakra point (seven in all).

The chakra points and their colours

Colour: Green
Chakra: Heart
Body part: Heart
Attributes: Healing, growth

Colour: Blue
Chakra: Throat
Body part: Throat
Attribute: Communication

Colour: Indigo
Chakra: Third eye
Body part: Forehead
Attribute: Intuition

Colour: Yellow
Chakra: Solar plexus
Body part: Digestive system
Attributes: Intellect, ego

Colour: Orange
Chakra: Abdomen
Body part: Reproductive organs
Attributes: Sexuality, reproduction

Colour: Red
Chakra: Root
Body parts: Waste system, lower limbs
Attributes: Security, life force

Colour: Violet
Chakra: Crown
Body part: Brain
Attribute: Higher spirit

Red

Red is a passionate, fiery colour that rules Tuesday and the planet Mars. It is associated with the astrological sign Aries, as well as fire, fast action and driving forces. It evokes anger, passion, courage, lust, love and career ambitions. Physically, it arouses strength, vibrancy, sexual vigour and health. Red can symbolize the archetypal god in magic.

Pink

While red is the colour of passion, pink is the true colour of romantic love. The colour pink rules Friday and the planet Venus. It is associated with all things romantic and positive, including good will, peace, affection, emotionally mature partnerships, caring, nurturing, successful marriage and emotional health. It is connected to Libra and Taurus.

Orange

Orange is a secondary colour of the sun. It is quite an adaptable colour and is associated with many things. For the most part, it is connected to ambition and the business world. Its primary associations are career goals, property deals, selling and success. It is associated with self-confidence, strength, justice and encouragement, but also with ego, pride and materialism.

Red Flowers
If you are casting a love spell, you can use red or pink rose petals to imbue your goal with the energy of the plant and its colour.

Pink Glass
The colour of pink glass actually comes from the mineral gold, so make sure that the properties of gold will also enhance your goal when using pink glass.

Red Stones
- Ruby
- Garnet
- Fire agate
- Red coral
- Red jasper
- Bloodstone

Pink Stones
- Pink diamond
- Pink tourmaline
- Pink topaz
- Rose quartz
- Rhodochrosite
- Pink opal
- Petalite
- Pink sapphire

Orange Stones
- Carnelian
- Fire opal
- Orange calcite
- Sunstone
- Orange topaz
- Coral
- Amber
- Plume agate
- Polished copper

Yellow

Yellow is a secondary sun colour. It is associated with intellectual pursuits and the mind, especially learning, intelligence, long-term memory and philosophy. Physically, it is connected to the nervous system. Emotionally, it is related to attraction, charm, persuasion and confidence. You can also call on yellow for protection. Although not directly related to the other attributes, you can use yellow to kindle the imagination.

Yellow Stones
- Yellow diamond
- Yellow topaz
- Citrine
- Cat's eye
- Lemon quartz
- Honey calcite

Gold

Gold is the primary colour of the sun and Sunday. It symbolizes an archetypal god representing all gods and all things masculine. In addition, time and culture have imbued it with associations to wealth and winning. It is connected to the astrological sign Leo.

Gold Paint
You can use gold paint to decorate containers of wealth, like a change jar, to attract prosperity.

Gold Stones
If you need to work magic with gold, a small gold nugget or piece of solid gold jewellery is the obvious choice.

Silver

Silver is the colour of the archetypal goddess representing all goddesses. It is connected to the moon and Monday. Silver is primarily associated with all things feminine, as well as intuition and psychic abilities. It is also associated with the astrological sign Cancer.

Psychic Powers
To enhance your psychic powers or meditations, you can carry a piece of silver. Pure silver jewellery is best, especially if it is also set with a moonstone, but you can also use a silver nugget or a pure silver coin (not modern alloy coins).

Silver Stones
Silver stones are difficult to find, but you can try:
- Grey pearl
- Galena
- Polished hematite

Green

Green is the colour of the earth and the earth mother. It is a symbol of harmony, fertility and prosperity. Fertility can take many forms, including conception, plant fertility and career fertility. Green is also a colour of prosperity in feng shui. If you are attempting to attract financial fertility, banknotes that feature the colour green are a powerful source. Of course, thanks to the Irish, green is also connected to luck.

Green Stones
- Malachite
- Emerald
- Jade
- Aventurine
- Green calcite
- Peridot
- Green tourmaline
- Moss agate
- Serpentine

Blue

Blue is the colour of communication and healing. It is connected to Thursday, Jupiter, Sagittarius and Pisces. Its gently moving, tranquil energy inspires you spiritually and creatively. Wearing blue can make you feel calm and patient. It soothes children and assists in falling asleep. Most of all, blue heals emotional wounds connected to communication. In the business world, blue is associated with trust and confidence, so it is often used in bank logos.

Blue Stones
- Turquoise
- Aquamarine
- Lapis lazuli
- Sapphire
- Angelite
- Blue apatite
- Blue lace agate

Purple

Purple is associated with spirituality, because it is the colour of the third eye (indigo). It is also connected with power, because it was the colour favoured by kings in history. Today, purple is associated with high-powered people, ambition and self-assurance. On the flipside, it is associated with psychic abilities and hidden knowledge. Purple is the colour of Wednesday and the planet Mercury. It is also associated with Gemini and Virgo.

Purple Stones
- Amethyst
- Fluorite
- Azurite

Brown

Brown is the colour of nature, but is associated more with animals than plants. It is, however, related to the woods and wilderness areas. It is a neutral colour, as well as a gentle banishing colour. Use brown to stop someone from harming you without cutting them from your life completely.

Black

Black is associated with protecting and banishing. It has long been affiliated with the 'dark side' – that is, all aspects of life that are difficult, harmful or evil. However, it is also the colour of Saturday and the god Saturn, who protects the home. It is connected to Capricorn and Aquarius.

White

White is both the absence of colour and the combination of all colours. If you cannot find a particular colour candle for a spell, choose white as a stand-in. It is a symbol of the goddess in her purest form, as well as a symbol of childhood, motherhood and pure love. It is an innocent colour associated with peace, the higher self, sincerity and truth.

Brown Stones
Brown crystals are unusual, but you can use:
- Tiger's eye
- Petrified wood

Black Stones
Black stones are enormously powerful, and have been used to form weapons and power objects for millennia.
- Obsidian
- Jet
- Black onyx

White Stones
White stones can be truly white, clear or cloudy. Popular ones include:
- Quartz
- White topaz
- White diamond
- White sapphire
- White calcite
- White selenite

STONES AND CRYSTALS

The earth produces a wide variety of crystals, gems and magical stones. As well as being used for their colour energy, they are also vessels of the earth's energy. Each type of stone possesses unique properties suitable for different kinds of spells; those described here are useful for a wide range of goals. Perform a cleansing ritual before using stones in magic.

Cleansing Stones and Crystals

Crystals and stones are powerful magnifiers of the earth's energy. They are also known to collect human energy and store it. If they store too much of it, they can break. After a period of heavy use, or following the successful completion of a spell, cleanse your stones and crystals by leaving them on a bed of rock salt for three days. If possible, set them out in the light of the full moon, too.

Quartz

Quartz has as many uses as it does colours. It is also a very affordable crystal. You can find quartz crystals in New Age shops, nature shops and even museum gift shops. They come both polished and unpolished, and in a variety of shapes and sizes. Choose the one that suits your purpose best. The most popular types of quartz are rose (love spells) and smoky (protection). Some types of quartz go under other names. Amethyst, citrine, tiger's eye, agate, aventurine and carnelian are all forms of quartz.

Agate

Agate is a type of quartz, but also comes in many forms itself. Tiger's eye and carnelian are two of the most common forms known by other names. For every purpose, there is a type of agate. You can often find agate consisting of several banded colours. Some of the more common forms and purposes are:

- Tiger's eye – prosperity
- Indian – protection
- Dendritic – travel
- Banded – healing
- Moss – cleansing, purification
- Fire – passion, sexuality
- Blue lace – mental balance

Carnelian

Carnelian is a red or orange form of agate, which also makes it a form of quartz. It is most powerful for career or ambition spells. It stirs the passions and enlivens the spirit. If you are looking for a new job, carry carnelian in your pocket to boost your confidence and charm during interviews.

Incorporating Stones into Magic

- Wear stones as jewellery — rose quartz has long been associated with love, and you will often find it carved into the shape of a heart, perfect for wearing as a pendant or brooch.
- Dress stones with magical oil during a spell, then carry them with you afterwards.
- Use them as divination tools for scrying.
- Add stones to an altar.

Onyx

Onyx is a black stone that is frequently found among ancient Egyptian artefacts. It is a stone of protection, especially psychic protection. You will often see it carved into small pyramids or other polished forms. It is rarely seen unpolished. It is connected to the root chakra (see page 17), and may be used to ground a person suffering from mental or physical imbalance.

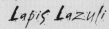

Lapis Lazuli

Lapis lazuli is a blue stone associated with healing and psychic knowledge. It was prized in ancient Egypt, where it was considered a holy gem. The Romans believed it to be an aphrodisiac. Renaissance painters ground it into a brilliant blue paint. If you wish to use it to improve meditation or scrying, stare into a polished stone. You can also buy a small piece to hold while meditating. Good lapis is expensive, but a small sliver carries enormous magical power.

Amber

Amber is a shape-shifting stone. It is actually a resin fossil; it is formed from organic matter, but is not made of sap. You can occasionally find a piece with an insect frozen inside. Copal is a softer form of amber. Most amber is yellowish orange, but it can run to deep brown. Other colours, such as red, green and blue, can occur, but are rare and expensive. Amber is associated with fire, because it burns, and is also a powerful healing stone. When left by the bed, it can arouse love or soothe nightmares.

Topaz

Topaz comes in a variety of colours. In general, it is a balancing and healing stone. Blue topaz arouses feelings of contentment and peace, while yellow topaz fills you with warmth and abundance.

HERBS

Herbs have enormous magical power. They hold the earth's energy within them, and each herb has unique properties that can enhance your magical goal. Herbs may also have medicinal properties; you can choose to draw on either aspect when performing a spell. There are as many herbs as there are purposes, but the herbs described here are excellent multi-taskers for use in spells.

Buying Herbs for Potions
When buying herbs for potions and other magical purposes, make sure that you buy food-grade herbs. Many herbs found in New Age shops are not safe for consumption, and may contain chemicals that could interfere with your magic. For the best herbs, find a natural food shop that sells food-grade herbs in bulk. Ask the herbalist on staff for advice if you need help.

Tools for Herbs
If possible, keep a special set of equipment for preparing herbs for magical use, instead of your everyday kitchen tools.

Incorporating Herbs into Spells

Herbs are easy to include in your spells, and you can do so with a variety of methods:

❀ Burn herbs as incense. You can buy incense sticks or cones, or burn loose herbs on charcoal discs, which can be found in most New Age shops. Always hold the disc with tongs when lighting it, and then place it in a heatproof container.

❀ Brew edible herbs into a tea or infusion, or add them to food that you have specially prepared with your magical goal in mind.

❀ Apply herbs to the skin as a poultice or lotion, or sprinkle them into a warm bath.

❀ During spells, sprinkle loose herbs into a burning cauldron or onto a fire (take care with safety). Use essential oils to dress candles and anoint stones.

❀ Dry herbs and carry them with you in a pouch.

Harvesting Herbs

If you grow your own herbs for magic, make sure that you grow them without chemicals and then harvest them correctly.

1 Harvest herbs after the sun has dried the dew, but before the major heat of the day sets in.

2 Always use a sharp magical knife to cut them. The tool should be consecrated specifically for this purpose (see pages 58–59).

3 Thank the plant for its gift and offer it something in return, such as a crystal, water or some soil.

4 Only harvest the amount you need, except in the autumn when you should take a large harvest to ensure healthy growth for the following year.

Rosemary
Rosemary has many uses in magic and is delicious in food. Kitchen rosemary can be used in magic, but you can also find it as incense or an essential oil. Its primary associations are:
• Healing
• Protection
• Love
• Purification
• Strength
• Stress relief
• Memory
• Mental clarity
• The sun
• Leo

Thyme
Thyme is another common kitchen herb that also has numerous magical properties. You can use it in cooking, burn it as incense, use the leaves in poultices and teas, or buy it as an essential oil. Thyme's associations include:
• Healing
• Love
• Psychic knowledge
• Purification
• Mercury
• Venus
• Water
• Taurus and Libra

Lavender
Lavender is used in some cooking, but is more typically found in drawer sachets and dream pillows. It can also be used loose, as incense or as an essential oil. Lavender's associations are:
• Happiness
• Love
• Protection
• Beauty
• Purification
• Relaxation
• Sleep
• Psychic knowledge
• Mercury
• Air
• Gemini and Virgo

Mugwort

Mugwort is primarily associated with psychic awareness, and is often used in scrying. It contains a toxic ingredient, so be careful with it in essential oil form. Its associations are:

• Divination
• Visions
• Intuition
• Healing
• Protection
• The earth
• Libra

Cedar

Cedar is a wood commonly found in closets, because it repels pests, but it also has magical properties. It is associated with:

• Prosperity
• Healing
• Purification
• Protection
• The sun
• Fire
• Aries and Sagittarius

Sandalwood statue of the Hindu god Ganesha, the guardian of the household.

Sandalwood

Sandalwood is one of the hippie herbs that have been reclaimed by Witches. It is usually used as incense, but is also available as an essential oil. It is primarily associated with:

• Healing
• Protection
• Harmony
• Purification
• Spirituality
• The sun and moon
• Water
• Cancer, Leo and Pisces

Cinnamon

Cinnamon is both spice and herb. Be very careful when working with loose cinnamon or cinnamon oil; avoid contact with the eyes and use it sparingly on the skin. Its associations are:

• Love
• Prosperity
• Passion
• Lust
• Healing
• Psychic knowledge
• Protection
• Purification
• The sun
• Fire
• Aries and Leo

Cinquefoil

Cinquefoil is also known as five-finger grass. It is mainly used for prosperity spells; simply toss some of the loose herb onto burning parchment to boost the spell's effectiveness. Its associations are:

• Prosperity
• Psychic knowledge
• Protection
• Jupiter

Patchouli

Although patchouli is typically associated with the hippies of the 1960s, it is actually a very powerful magical herb. It is most commonly used as incense, but can also be used loose or as an essential oil. It is connected to:

- Lust
- Prosperity
- Protection
- Saturn and the earth
- Taurus, Aquarius and Capricorn

Frankincense

Frankincense is a resin that is usually burned, but can also be found in essential oil form. Many Witches use it during seasonal rituals or as a stand-in for other incenses. Be careful with it in enclosed rooms, because it produces a billowy white smoke. Its associations are:

- Psychic awareness
- Purification
- Protection
- Spirituality
- Healing
- Divination
- Fire
- Aries and Sagittarius

Special Properties of Resins

Resins, such as amber and frankincense, are part-herb and part-stone. The softer resins, such as frankincense, are burned as incense. Amber, a harder resin, is used as a stone (see page 23). Most resins can also be turned into essential oils.

Rose

Rose is the ultimate love herb. Its scent is an aphrodisiac, and it has been the focus of love poems and romantic gifts for centuries. In addition to this steeping in romantic lore, the plant itself has powerful magical properties. To use it in a love spell, you can add a drop of food-safe rose oil to a meal, anoint candles, stones or your skin with oil, bathe in petal-filled water, burn dried rose petals or even eat the petals themselves. Roses are associated with:

- Love
- Beauty
- Lust
- Healing
- Luck
- Psychic knowledge (especially of future loves)
- Venus
- Water
- Taurus, Cancer, Libra and Sagittarius

Rose and Jasmine Oils

These oils are expensive. Fortunately, they are also potent. Usually, a single drop is sufficient for any spell. Keep the bottles in a refrigerator to prevent evaporation. As an inexpensive alternative, steep fresh rose petals or jasmine flowers in jojoba oil for three days.

Jasmine

Jasmine is one of the ultimate aphrodisiacs. Its flower is the most potent part of the plant and can be burned, drunk as tea, incorporated into lotion or used as an essential oil. If you are taking a warm bath, sprinkle some of the flowers in the water. Jasmine is associated with:

- Love
- Lust
- Passion
- Psychic knowledge
- Emotions
- Prosperity
- Dreams
- Spirituality
- The moon
- Water
- Cancer and Pisces

The Magic of the Heavens

For as long as humans have been able to observe the transits of the planets, sun and moon through the skies, these heavenly bodies have been associated with magic and superstition. According to astrology, their position at birth affects our personalities. They also affect daily life and add enormous magical power to spells.

The Sun

- The sun determines the length of the day, gives us life and lights our way. It and the moon were the first heavenly bodies that could be observed to affect life.
- The sun represents the god, and is associated with traditional masculine pursuits. Beware that its energy can be domineering, overbearing and arrogant.

The Sun's Magical Associations
- Health
- Success
- Career goals
- Ambition
- Money and wealth
- Law
- Buying and selling
- Strength
- Leadership
- Men's mysteries
- Children

Mercury

- Mercury is the closest planet to the sun, and travels swiftly around it, which is probably how it came to be associated with the fleet-footed god Mercury.
- Mercury's assistance can be inconsistent, so look to balance its negative properties with another planet's more peaceful energy.

Mercury's Magical Associations
- Communication
- Travel
- Intellect and learning
- Mental perception
- Teaching
- Writing
- Creativity
- Memory
- Cleverness
- Reasoning
- Arguments
- Sarcasm and cynicism
- Trickery and thievery

The Sun
After the moon, the sun is the most powerful heavenly body in magic.

Venus

• Venus is the planet between Mercury and the earth. It is warmer than the earth, but some speculate that it was once earth-like.
• Venus is commonly associated with women, although women are ruled by the moon. It is most usually associated with traditionally feminine concepts. The symbol for woman and the symbol for Venus are the same.
• In addition to the goddess Venus, the planet is ruled by the goddess Frigg.

Mars

• Mars lies on the other side of the earth. It appears to us as dark orange or fiery red. As a counterbalance to Venus, it is associated with masculinity, especially dark masculinity.
• Ruled by the war god Mars, it is also associated with the Germanic god Tyr. The symbol for man and the symbol for Mars are the same.
• Mars is not simply masculine energy. It is a very aggressive masculine energy, as compared to the gentler fatherly energy of the sun.

Jupiter

- Jupiter is the largest body in the heavens, so it is fitting that it is named after the king of the gods. In Germanic beliefs, it is associated with Thor.
- Although it is a masculine planet, Jupiter's energy is more intellectual and regal than the fiery energy of Mars or the fatherly energy of the sun.
- If you are performing a spell related to justice or business, then the hour of Jupiter on Thursday is your best choice.

Jupiter's Magical Associations
- Truth
- Knowledge
- Religion
- Education
- Language
- Foreign countries
- Faith
- Philosophy
- Publication
- Reading
- Banking
- Judgement
- Justice
- Optimism
- Compassion
- Law and legal action
- Politics
- Leadership
- Honour
- Public acclaim
- Wealth
- Business
- Responsibility
- Conceit
- Self-indulgence
- Excessive optimism

Saturn

- Saturn was the final visible planet in the ancient world, and is therefore the last planet with a large number of associations.
- It is another masculine planet, ruled by the god Saturn, who is the only Roman god with a day named after him.
- Saturn's energy is protective, and is often used for spells to protect the home from intruders. However, its distance makes it aloof, which can create limitations.

Saturn's Magical Associations
- Tenacity
- Law
- Dentistry
- Construction
- Real estate
- Thriftiness
- Reliability
- Self-discipline
- Patience
- History and time
- Order
- Slow change
- Inhibition
- Intolerance
- Dogmatism
- Depression
- Obstacles
- Isolation

Uranus's Magical Associations

- Eccentric ideas
- Inventiveness
- Electricity
- Bizarre occurrences
- Reform
- Unexpected change

Uranus

- Uranus is named after the father of Jupiter and Saturn. Its qualities reflect its strangeness. Unlike the other planets, its axis is turned to the side and it rolls rather than spins.
- Its influence on spells is weaker than that of the visible planets. Uranus does not have a day of the week or a planetary hour (see pages 34–35), so use a stone or herb associated with it to invoke its properties.

Neptune's Magical Associations

- Dreams
- Visions
- Ideal
- Fantasy
- Art
- Healing
- Illusion
- Psychic knowledge
- Alchemy

Neptune

- Neptune is named after the god of the sea, and is therefore mostly associated with watery qualities.
- It has fewer properties than the seven major planets, but it still has some influence on us.

Pluto's Magical Associations

- Bringing order from chaos
- Group ideas
- Rapid manifestation
- Uniting
- Disrupting

Dwarf Planets and Asteroids

Pluto
Although scientists have downgraded Pluto from planet to dwarf planet, it still possesses magical importance. Like the other two outlying planets, Uranus and Neptune, it has fewer associations, but it can be a powerful magical tool. Pluto is an eccentric planet, travelling on an elliptical path rather than a circular orbit. Its path sometimes passes within that of Neptune, and it has a tendency to shuffle the order of the planets.

Ceres
Ceres is another dwarf planet. Its small size gives it much less magical influence than Pluto. Its magical associations include reproduction, fertility, pregnancy and motherhood.

Asteroids
Juno, Pallas Athena and Chiron are asteroids charted in astrology, but they have never been considered planets. Their energy is fleeting in magic and they have few associations.

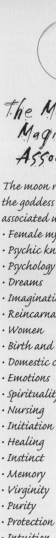

The MOON

The moon is the most important heavenly body to consider when casting spells. It exerts enormous influence over the earth, governing the tides, crops and certain aspects of the human body, and therefore has a strong influence on magic. By monitoring the moon's phases and being aware of its transit through the heavens, you can cast a spell to use the moon to its best advantage.

The Moon's Magical Associations

The moon represents the goddess and is associated with:

- Female mysteries
- Psychic knowledge
- Psychology
- Dreams
- Imagination
- Reincarnation
- Women
- Birth and children
- Domestic concerns
- Emotions
- Spirituality
- Nursing
- Initiation
- Healing
- Instinct
- Memory
- Virginity
- Purity
- Protection
- Intuition
- Beauty

Moon Phases

The moon goes through four phases each lunar cycle. The total cycle is 29.5 days. The phases are:

New Moon
The new moon is best for spells relating to beginning new things. If you plan to do a multi-day spell with a positive goal in mind, then you could start on the new moon and work forwards.

Waxing Moon
The moon waxes from the new moon to the full moon. The waxing moon is a period of growth and newness. Cast spells to attract, create, inspire or produce.

Full Moon
The full moon is the most magical night of the month. Its energy can be used for love, knowledge, protection, prosperity, divination and numerous other goals. Witches celebrate the full moon with a ritual known as the esbat, which honours the goddess.

Waning Moon
The moon wanes from the full moon to the dark moon. The waning moon is a period of dying off. Cast spells to remove, banish or release.

Pearls and Selenite
Incorporate these stones into your spells to amplify the influence of the moon.

Moon Names

Historically, each moon of the year has had a name. The names vary, depending on the natural cycle and traditions of the local culture. These are an example:

January	Wolf Moon
February	Snow Moon
March	Worm Moon
April	Pink Moon
May	Flower Moon
June	Strawberry Moon
July	Mead Moon
August	Red Moon
September	Harvest Moon
October	Blood Moon
November	Frost Moon
December	Cold Moon

A waxing moon just after a new moon.

Blue Moon

Until 1946, the blue moon was the third full moon in any season with four full moons. A 1946 error in *Sky & Telegraph* magazine resulted in the modern belief that the blue moon is the second full moon in a single month. Blue moons are often a result of time-zone shifts. Although it is full on the 31st night of the month in one place, it may not be full until the 1st night of the month in another place. Most Witches do not accord any additional power to a blue moon.

Full Moon
A view of the full moon in the northern hemisphere. The moon appears upside-down in the southern hemisphere, with the crater at the top.

Dark Moon

Some Witches work with the dark moon in addition to the moon phases. Some consider it to be another name for the new moon. Others consider it to be the last three days before the new lunar cycle begins. In their view, the new moon occurs at the moment when the sun and moon are conjunct (aligned on the same side of the earth, so that the side of the moon usually visible from the earth is not illuminated by the sun). Others believe that the dark moon continues until the first crescent of the moon is visible, when it becomes the new moon.

PLANETARY DAYS AND HOURS

Each day of the week, and each hour of the day and night, is associated with a planet. By performing spells on a specific day and during a particular hour, you can harness the energy of the planets that are associated with your goal. Of course, you can perform a spell at any time and it will be effective if your intention is pure.

Astronomical Clock
This medieval clock in Prague in the Czech Republic displays a variety of astronomical information. The outer dial indicates the standard 24 hours; the curved golden lines indicate the variable planetary hours.

Calculating Planetary Hours

The first hour of each day begins with the planet that rules that day, then the hours rotate through the other visible planets. Determine the planetary hours as follows:

1. Find the sunrise, sunset and sunrise times for a 24-hour period where you live.
2. Make a chart for daylight hours 1–12 and night-time hours 1–12, starting at the first sunrise. Sunset marks the start of night.
3. Calculate the number of minutes in the day and in the night. Divide each by 12 to determine the length of each 'hour'.
4. Note the start time of each hour in your 24-hour chart.
5. Compare your chart to the hour charts opposite to find the hour associated with each planet.

Example
Monday, 8 December 2008, in Los Angeles, California, sunrise is at 6:18, sunset is at 5:11, and the next sunrise is at 6:19. The day is 10 hours and 53 minutes, or 653 minutes, and the night is 13 hours and 8 minutes, or 788 minutes. When divided by 12, each day hour is just over 54 minutes. Each night hour is almost 66 minutes. The chart should appear like so:

Day:
Hour 1 begins at 6:18 = Moon
Hour 2 begins at 7:12 = Saturn

Night:
Hour 1 begins at 5:11 = Venus
Hour 2 begins at 6:17 = Mercury

Planetary Hours of the Day and Night

Hour	Sunday	Monday	Tuesday	Wednesday	Thursday	Friday	Saturday
1	Sun	Moon	Mars	Mercury	Jupiter	Venus	Saturn
2	Venus	Saturn	Sun	Moon	Mars	Mercury	Jupiter
3	Mercury	Jupiter	Venus	Saturn	Sun	Moon	Mars
4	Moon	Mars	Mercury	Jupiter	Venus	Saturn	Sun
5	Saturn	Sun	Moon	Mars	Mercury	Jupiter	Venus
6	Jupiter	Venus	Saturn	Sun	Moon	Mars	Mercury
7	Mars	Mercury	Jupiter	Venus	Saturn	Sun	Moon
8	Sun	Moon	Mars	Mercury	Jupiter	Venus	Saturn
9	Venus	Saturn	Sun	Moon	Mars	Mercury	Jupiter
10	Mercury	Jupiter	Venus	Saturn	Sun	Moon	Mars
11	Moon	Mars	Mercury	Jupiter	Venus	Saturn	Sun
12	Saturn	Sun	Moon	Mars	Mercury	Jupiter	Venus

Hour	Sunday	Monday	Tuesday	Wednesday	Thursday	Friday	Saturday
1	Jupiter	Venus	Saturn	Sun	Moon	Mars	Mercury
2	Mars	Mercury	Jupiter	Venus	Saturn	Sun	Moon
3	Sun	Moon	Mars	Mercury	Jupiter	Venus	Saturn
4	Venus	Saturn	Sun	Moon	Mars	Mercury	Jupiter
5	Mercury	Jupiter	Venus	Saturn	Sun	Moon	Mars
6	Moon	Mars	Mercury	Jupiter	Venus	Saturn	Sun
7	Saturn	Sun	Moon	Mars	Mercury	Jupiter	Venus
8	Jupiter	Venus	Saturn	Sun	Moon	Mars	Mercury
9	Mars	Mercury	Jupiter	Venus	Saturn	Sun	Moon
10	Sun	Moon	Mars	Mercury	Jupiter	Venus	Saturn
11	Venus	Saturn	Sun	Moon	Mars	Mercury	Jupiter
12	Mercury	Jupiter	Venus	Saturn	Sun	Moon	Mars

Tip: Avoid an excessive amount of one particular energy by casting a spell on the day associated with one planet and the hour of a different planet that will also enhance the spell.

WHEN TO AVOID MAGIC

There are numerous opportunities to cast spells at a beneficial time, but you should also be aware of certain days or times when magic should be avoided, if possible. Spells can have an unexpected or undesired result when the moon is void of course or Mercury is retrograde. The effects of other retrograde planets should also be considered, but will have less of an impact.

Moon

Mercury Retrograde

Mercury has a shorter year than the earth, so it appears to move backwards, or retrograde, through the sky at several points during the year. Mercury retrograde can have an unexpected effect on spells. These periods are also rife with interpersonal tension, disrupted communications, disrupted travel, traffic jams and electronics breakdowns. Mercury retrograde typically lasts 3 weeks, and occurs 3–4 times a year.

Mercury

Moon Void of Course

Each month, the moon travels through each of the astrological signs. The time when it is between signs is called void of course. These periods can last from 1 minute to more than 24 hours; most last 2–3 hours. Try to avoid casting any spells when the moon is VOC. Emergency spells can be cast, but be careful with your phrasing. A moon VOC can disrupt or prevent your desired result.

Things to Avoid
When Mercury is retrograde, avoid casting any spell that is not an emergency, such as signing contracts, beginning new projects, beginning or ending a relationship, or making any other major decision. Decisions or agreements made during a Mercury retrograde tend to be shortlived.

Things to Do
Mercury retrograde is an excellent time to be creative or to brainstorm. During this time, you should write, create art or come up with new ideas that you will put into effect once the retrograde is over.

Other Retrograde Planets

The other planets may also go retrograde at some point during the year. For most of these planets, their retrograde periods can last several months. Fortunately, the effects of these other retrogrades are relatively minor.

Venus Retrograde: Slowing down of relationships, less appreciation of art and beauty. Avoid getting married or ending a relationship during a Venus retrograde.

Mars Retrograde: Increases in anger and war, greater tendency towards introspection, reassessment of major projects and contracts. Once again, avoid making a major relationship decision or engaging in a major business negotiation.

Jupiter Retrograde: Increased spirituality and philosophical exploration. Avoid starting new businesses, except for non-profit or community service organizations.

Saturn Retrograde: Renegotiation and reassessment of projects and agreements. You might also reassess your own path through life. Avoid starting new businesses.

Uranus Retrograde: New discoveries, inventiveness, rebelliousness. Control impulsive urges, or you may have to undo your actions later.

Neptune Retrograde: Tendency towards delusion, but also an increase in perceptiveness. Resolve issues that are revealed during this period to prevent them from intensifying later.

Pluto Retrograde: Greater insight and a willingness to release old attachments and illusions. Now is the time to remove outmoded ideas or cleanse your body and spirit.

The Solar System
Planets can appear to move backwards when their position changes in relation to the earth as they orbit the sun.

Astrological Calendars
The best way to determine the lunar and planetary transits for any given day is to buy an astrological calendar specific to your time zone and hemisphere.

DiVine Magic

Witches believe in the ancient gods and goddesses, who are still present today. Each deity is associated with one or more aspects of life, from war to the weather. In addition to worshipping them as divine beings, we ask the gods associated with our goals to help us when performing spells. There are thousands of gods from many cultures to choose from.

Common Pantheons
Each culture had its own pantheon of deities with magical associations. The most common pantheons worshipped by Witches are described on the following pages, but the spells in Chapter 3 also include deities from less well-known pantheons that you may wish to invoke.

Egyptian Temple of Anubis

Which Pantheon?

- Some Witches are eclectic, which means that they work with whichever deity is appropriate to their purpose, regardless of pantheon. Others are drawn to one single pantheon.

- Depending on your heritage or affinities, you could choose to work with a lesser known group of deities, such as the Aztec or Finnish gods. There are numerous options, not just those described in this book.

- You are not limited to a pantheon associated with your heritage in this life. It is possible that you were from a different culture in a past life and may still feel an affiliation with those old gods.

Matron and Patron Deities
Once you have been working with the gods for a long time, you may notice that you feel particularly drawn to one god and one goddess. These are your Matron and Patron deities. They will shepherd you through your life and offer guidance and support when you need it. Get to know them through meditation, spellwork and prayer.

Although you may choose to invoke deities from different pantheons at different times, avoid calling deities from different pantheons in the same spell. Greek and Roman deities are assimilated today, but calling a Celtic god with a Hindu goddess could cause trouble.

Choosing a Pantheon to Work With

If you want to work with a single pantheon, follow these steps to find the right one:

1. Read about all the various pantheons. Research their mythology and lore in detail. If one appeals to you most, focus on that one.

2. Research your bloodline in this life. Find out how many cultures are mingled in your family tree.

3. Meditate and ask the gods to bring you a message. Members of one pantheon might make regular appearances.

4. If you do not feel comfortable meditating, you can ask the gods to come to you in your sleep. Just after getting into bed, invite them to visit you. Write down the images you remember when you first wake, then look for those symbols or images in your research.

5. Once you have found a pantheon that resonates with you, meditate on each of the gods to make sure that you are comfortable with them. Make offerings to them as well.

Venus

The Mother Goddess
Early archaeologists reported that ancient cultures worshipped a single goddess known as the Great Mother. Modern scholars have since disproven this theory. However, many pantheons include a goddess who gave birth to many of the other gods or to the earth itself. Witches today often call on the Great Mother or the Mother Goddess, and consider her to be the essence of the feminine divine and the earth.

CELTIC DEITIES

The Celtic gods and goddesses were prevalent throughout Western and Southern Europe. Records of them have been found in Ireland, England, France and Northern Italy. Although there are over 300 Celtic deities, most of them are minor local gods. Most modern Witches work with the primary gods that were known throughout most of the Celtic lands.

The Celtic Heirarchy
Legend states that Ireland was settled by a series of invaders. The first were the Tuatha de Danaan, the people of the goddess Danu. They fled following later invasions, and then returned to conquer again. They were finally defeated by the Milesians and then intermarried with them. The majority of the Celtic deities descend from the Tuatha de Danaan.

Raven's feather to signify the Morrigan.

Triple Goddesses

The number three was important in Celtic beliefs. As a result, some of their goddesses are triads.

Brighid is probably the most prominent of all the Celtic deities today. In ancient times, she was worshipped throughout the Celtic lands, even after they were conquered by the Romans. She is known as St Brigit in Christian lore. The monastery at Kildare kept a perpetual fire burning in her honour for centuries. As a Celtic goddess, Brighid is one of the triple goddesses. All three of her aspects are called Brighid, and they are considered to be sisters. One sister is the patroness of culture, fertility and healing. The second is the patroness of poetry, inspiration, divination and bardic lore. The third sister is the patroness of fire and smithcraft.

The Morrigan is a triple goddess; the names of her three aspects vary, according to different traditions. Her different aspects are associated with crows or ravens, and panic or frenzy. As a triad, they are considered war and death goddesses, but also goddesses of fertility. A Celtic myth describes the Samhain (31 October) night when she mated with the Daghdha while straddling the banks of the River Unius and washing bloody corpses and the armour of those fated to die in an upcoming battle.

St Brigit of Kildare
This stained glass window depicts the Christian version of the Celtic goddess Brighid.

Celtic Gods

Manannan Mac Lir is one of the earliest Celtic gods, considered older than the Tuatha de Danaan. He is the god of the sea, specifically the sea around the Isle of Man off the northwest coast of England, and rules the weather. He is also associated with reincarnation. He is the foster father of the god Lugh.

The Daghdha is considered the father of the Irish gods and one of three kings of the Tuatha de Danaan. His name is usually translated as 'the good god'. The druids considered him the god of wisdom, a sky god and an earth god. He carries a club and possesses a cauldron of perpetual nourishment. He is the father of Brighid, Ogma and Aengus.

Lugh is the god of light and skills. Some myths say that he came from across the sea, while others say he is a son of the Daghdha. He is the keeper of a great spear and was a god of many skills. He is the second great king of the Tuatha de Danaan, and granted his men magical skill in battle. His primary festival is the harvest celebration of Lughnasadh, which falls on 1 August.

Ogma is the god of the word. He guides the dead, but also has the power to bind men with his words. He is the father of the Celtic alphabet known as Ogham, a religious alphabet not typically used for everyday communication. He is associated with the god Ogmios, who is the Gaulish god of eloquence and poetry.

Aengus is a son of the Daghdha and the god of unrequited love. He is also associated with funerary rites. As a trickster god, he is known for his wit and charm.

Cernunnos is a horned god of Gaulish origin. He wears the antlers of a stag and is a god of fertility and animals. He is a guardian of the otherworld, and is associated with prosperity. He is also connected with the god Herne, who is a god of hunting.

The Ogham Alphabet
The letters of the Ogham alphabet are composed of short lines along a central axis. Some Witches inscribe each letter onto a stick, and use the sticks for divination in a similar way to runes.

Ogma

Gundestrup Cauldron
Cernunnos is one of the Celtic deities depicted on the cauldron (see page 68). He is shown with antlers and is surrounded by animals.

TEUTONIC DEITIES

The Teutonic gods are a combination of both Germanic and Norse gods. The majority of Witches working with these gods consider them to be Norse deities. Most of their lore is found in two 13th-century Icelandic documents known as the Poetic Edda and the Prose Edda. They continue to be worshipped in Iceland as well as by modern Pagans known as Asatruar.

The Vanir and Æsir
The Norse pantheon is divided into two groups: the Æsir and the Vanir. The Æsir are associated with war, spirituality and intellectual interests. The Vanir are associated with nature, material pursuits and the emotions.

Gods and Goddesses of the Vanir

The deities of the Vanir are more feminine and associated with the home and family. They include:

Njord

Freya is the goddess of fertility, sex and love. She is the daughter of Njord and the wife/sister of Frey. She is also associated with seers and divination. Some myths co-mingle her with Frigga.

Frey is a rare fertility god, and a god of marriage. He is also a god of the earth, peace and the king of the dwarves. He possesses a magic ship that can hold all the Teutonic gods.

Njord is both a giant and a god of the sea, wind and storms. As ruler of the Vanir, he is associated with wealth, the weather and the harvest.

He and Frey live among the Æsir as part of a peace treaty between the two groups.

Ingwaz

Each rune is associated with a deity. For example, ingwaz is connected with Frey, and sowilu with Balder.

Sowilu

Gods and Goddesses of the Æsir

The deities of the Æsir are more masculine and associated with manly pursuits. Where there are two names, the first is from Norse mythology and the second from Germanic mythology.

Odin/Woden is associated with war, victory, wisdom and poetry. The word Wednesday is based on his name. He is the god of the Æsir who hung from the world tree, Yggdrasil, for nine days to receive the runes (see page 86), and rode Sleipnir, an eight-legged horse that could ride to the underworld.

Loki, a trickster god, is neither Æsir nor Vanir. He switches allegiance between the two to suit his own ends. He is associated with chaos. He is a thief who steals from the gods, but also occasionally rescues them from harm.

Tyr/Tiw is the god of battle, the law and the sky. He is a son of Odin and Frigga, and a brother to Balder. The word Tuesday derives from the name of this god of the Æsir.

Frigga, wife of Odin, is the goddess of the clouds and the queen of heaven. She is also associated with love and fertility. Friday is named after her.

Thor/Thunar is the god of thunder, and Thursday is named after him. He is also the god of the sky and the household, and a protector of man. He is often associated with fertility. He is known for his great hammer, called Mjollnir, that never misses its target, but also possesses a great axe. Like the other gods of the Æsir, his father is Odin. A giantess named Jörd was his mother, not Odin's wife, Frigga.

Odin riding Sleipnir

Balder, a son of Odin and Frigga, is a god of the sun and of innocence. He is called the 'good god' or the 'shining one'. According to the myths, he was tricked by Loki and died. He lives in the underworld and is forbidden to return from there until after Ragnorak, the Norse version of the apocalypse.

Thor's hammer formation in Bryce Canyon National Park, Utah, United States. Thor could flatten mountains with his mighty hammer.

EGYPTIAN DEITIES

Aside from the Greek and Roman gods, the Egyptian gods are probably the most researched and catalogued of all the pantheons. They also have an extensive following among modern Witches. Although their religious system was different from anything known today, their gods are still relevant to the concerns of Witches and are known to assist with modern spells.

Personification of the Gods

The gods of most pantheons were depicted in human form. The Egyptian gods were usually depicted with human legs and an animal head. Animals were highly venerated in Egypt, and each god is associated with an animal in addition to his or her other qualities. Although the animals themselves were not divine, they were connected to the divine.

Goddess of Life

Isis is sometimes depicted with wings, which she wraps around the dead while she breathes life back into them for the afterlife.

The Egyptian Pantheon

The Egyptian pantheon is not as highly ordered as most other pantheons. Many of the gods are part of a cycle, rather than connected through parentage and marriage. Although the pharaohs were considered gods, modern Witches do not worship the pharaohs; instead, we work with the primary deities.

Egyptian Goddesses

Isis is the mother goddess and the consort of Osiris. She is also his sister, and the sister of Set. Isis is usually depicted in human form wearing a crown shaped like a throne, or a sun disc surrounded by cow horns. She was said to protect the gods of Egypt as children, as well as wives and mothers.

Nut is the creator goddess and the mother of Osiris, Isis and Set. She is usually depicted as a cow hanging in the heavens. She is sometimes shown with the head of a cat.

Hathor is both a mother goddess and a goddess of love and sexuality. She is usually depicted as a cow or as a woman wearing a sun disc surrounded by cow horns. She is also associated with the sky and snakes. Her father is the sun god Ra. She was the mother of the pharaohs.

God of the Afterlife

Anubis is the funerary god of the Egyptian pantheon. In their culture, death was seen as a transition rather than an end. He stands next to the scale that weighs the heart to determine whether the deceased should be blessed or damned. He may be a son of Ra, Osiris or Set. He is associated with jackals and usually depicted as a man with a jackal's head or a dog's head.

Hathor is often depicted as a woman wearing a sun disc surrounded by cow horns.

Egyptian Gods

Osiris is considered to be the first king of Egypt, and is a god of the underworld, the law and the harvest. He is probably the most important god of the pantheon. He was murdered by his brother Set and thrown into the Nile. Isis found his body and breathed life back into him; she then conceived Horus with his semen. Set then cut his body into 14 pieces and scattered them throughout Egypt. Isis again found his parts and buried them. He is one of the few gods depicted in human form, and usually holds a crook and flail. He is also usually depicted in mummy form.

Set is the opposite of Osiris. Rather than noble, he is the god of the violent sea, evil and darkness. He is usually depicted with the head of an aardvark. Several pharaohs proclaimed themselves to serve under Set rather than the traditional Horus.

The Eye of Horus

Horus is the sky god who inhabits the body of the living pharaoh. He is usually depicted as a man with a falcon's head. His symbol is the Eye of Horus. He is also connected to the sun.

Ra is the sun god and a creator god. He has no father or mother, but created himself. He is also a god of the underworld. He is often depicted with a ram's head. He is also associated with cobras.

Anubis is the jackal-headed god of the underworld, associated with mummification and the afterlife.

Geb is another creator god, the husband/brother of Nut and the father of Osiris, Isis and Set. He is the god of the earth and of healing. He is said to have laid the egg from which the world sprang. He often appears in crocodile form.

GREEK AND ROMAN DEITIES

In addition to the surviving Classical literature, the myths and legends of the Greek and Roman deities were revived in Renaissance, Neoclassical and Romantic literature. Originally, the two pantheons were separate. However, Romans gradually assimilated the myths and associations of the Greek gods into their Latin gods, who had fewer myths surrounding them.

Greek Pantheon

The 12 universal gods of the Greek pantheon were known as the Olympians. Most of them lived on Mount Olympus, but were known to meddle in human affairs. The Olympians descended from the original gods, known as the Titans, who were overthrown by their children.

Greek and Roman Goddesses

Juno and Hera are the goddesses of marriage, women, fertility and family. They are married to Jupiter and Zeus, although Hera is also Zeus's sister. They are the mothers of Mars and Ares, and are associated with peacocks.

Minerva and Athena are the goddesses of warfare, wisdom, and arts and crafts. Athena sprang fully formed and wearing armour from the head of Zeus. That portion of the legend was also later assimilated to Minerva. They are associated with owls.

Diana and Artemis are the virgin goddesses of the hunt and the moon. They are associated with the bow and deer. Artemis is the daughter of Zeus and twin sister of Apollo.

Demeter is the Greek goddess of the harvest and fertility. Her daughter, Persephone, was kidnapped by Hades, the lord of the underworld. Winter occurs during the three months of the year when Persephone lives in the underworld.

Venus and Aphrodite are the goddesses of love, beauty and sexuality. Aphrodite was married to the blacksmith god Hephaestus, but had an affair with Ares. Ares and Aphrodite are the parents of Eros, the god of love and lust. Venus and Aphrodite are both associated with doves, and were born from the foam of the sea.

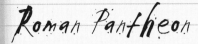

Zeus on a silver coin dating from 421–365 BC.

Neptune

Roman Pantheon

The Roman pantheon consists of two types of gods: primary deities and lares, or household spirits. The primary deities were remote from daily human life and usually required the intercession of a priest.

Greek and Roman Gods

Jupiter and Zeus are the kings of their respective pantheons. They are associated with thunder and the sky, and are brothers to Neptune and Poseidon, the sea gods. They are married to Juno and Hera. Zeus is the father of Artemis, Ares, Apollo, Athena, Hermes and, in some reports, Dionysus. Jupiter is the father of their Roman counterparts.

Mars and Ares are the gods of war and murder. They are associated with dogs and spears, and are the sons of Jupiter and Zeus. Ares is the father of Eros with Aphrodite.

Neptune and Poseidon are the gods of the sea and horses. They carry tridents and are associated with bulls.

Bacchus and Dionysus are the very popular gods of wine and revelry. Major festivals were held in their honour. Some legends report that

Dionysus is the son of Demeter and Zeus. Bacchus is the son of Jupiter. They are associated with the phallus, but are not fertility gods.

Mercury and Hermes are the fleet-footed messenger gods. They are associated with communication, commerce and travel. Hermes is something of a trickster god, and also plays a role in leading the dead to the underworld. He is associated with winged boots, and invented the lyre. Hermes is the son of Zeus, and Mercury is the son of Jupiter. Mercury is also associated with the wind.

Apollo is the Greek god of light, truth, poetry, music, healing and prophecy. He is associated with the sun, but is not the god of the sun. He is the twin brother of Artemis. He is also associated with the lyre. Rather than being readily accessible, he is a remote god.

The Wand of Hermes
Known as the Caduceus, the wand represents balance – heaven/earth, male/female, light/dark, good/evil.

Note: Where there are two names, the first is from Roman mythology and the second from Greek mythology.

CHINESE DEITIES

The Chinese gods worshipped by modern Witches are ancient deities modified by the legends of Confucianism, Taoism and Buddhism. The majority of the early gods were associated with nature, while later gods were associated with general concepts. The Chinese system is very different from most Western systems, but certain gods are very relatable to Western minds.

The Chinese Pantheon
The Chinese do not have a fixed pantheon like most Western pantheons. Instead, different mythologies place different gods at the top. Those described here are some of the more prominent.

The Eight Immortals

These Taoist deities were born human but became gods. They represent various aspects of life:

Cao Guojiu possesses a jade tablet that can cleanse the environment.

Han Xiangzi, a philosopher, is associated with a life-giving flute.

He Xiangu, the only goddess of the eight, is associated with health.

Lan Caihe may be male, female or both, but is usually a young male. He carries a basket of flowers associated with longevity.

Note: The spellings used here are approximate – converting Chinese characters into English is not an exact science.

Copy of ancient Chinese mural of 60 gods by Daozi Wu.

T'ien Hou is the goddess of fishing.

Other Prominent Chinese Deities

Kuan Yin is the goddess of mercy and peace, and the protector of women. She is second in importance to the Buddha. According to some legends, she was once human but is now a goddess. She is associated with the lotus flower.

The Jade Emperor is the supreme god of all the deities of Buddhism and Taoism. He is the god of purity, and the creator who tracks incarnations and rules every aspect of earthly life. In heaven, he is Yu Huang Shang Ti; on earth, he is the Jade Emperor. He is not directly involved in the lives of people, but rules remotely.

Hsi Wang Mu is the goddess of longevity and the underworld. She is one of the oldest Chinese deities. She was once a plague goddess, but was softened under Taoism. She determines the length of life and can grant immortality. She is often depicted as a tiger-toothed woman.

Tsao Chun is the kitchen and hearth god who is honoured by each household. He is a conduit to the Jade Emperor, because legend states that he travels to heaven each year to report on the members of the household.

T'ien Hou is the queen of heaven and the goddess of oceans and fresh water. She was born human and later elevated to goddesshood. She is second in power to the Jade Emperor. She is also associated with fishing and boats.

Monkey (Sun Wukong) is a trickster god. According to legend, he first visited the underworld to tear up his name and prevent his death. He then travelled to heaven. Buddha said that he could rule heaven if he could leap off Buddha's hand. Monkey leapt many miles, believing he had succeeded, only to discover he was still on Buddha's palm.

Li Tieguai attends to the poor, sick and needy.

Lu Dongbin, associated with wisdom and enlightenment, is also known to drink and philander.

Zhang Guolao, the oldest (in age) of the eight, is associated with health, wine and Qigong (a method of cultivating energy).

Zhong Quan, the leader of the eight, has a fan that can revive the dead.

African Deities

Most of the African gods come to us from the Yoruban and Dahomey regions of Nigeria, and are primarily worshipped by the followers of Vodun and Santeria. Some of the gods of the two religions are the same, while others have the same name but different attributes, or a different name for the same attribute. Other regions of Africa have their own gods, but they are not widely consulted outside of Africa.

Olorun

Both Santerians and Voduns believe in a supreme, unreachable god known as Olorun or Oludumare; in Vodun, he is also known as Nana Buluku. Olorun created the other deities — known as orishas in Santeria, and loas in Vodun — to interact with the people for him. There are seven major deities, plus several minor deities that can be called upon when the need arises. Obatalá/Obatala is Olorun's representative on earth. Olorun is associated with the colour white and the number 1.

Note: *Where there are two names, the first is the Santerian deity and the second is the Vodun deity. Colour and number associations are primarily Santerian, but some Vodun practitioners have also adopted them.*

The Major Deities

Obatalá/Obatala –
Obatalá is the lead god associated with fertility, purity and patience in Santeria. He is associated with white and the number 8. In Vodun, Obatala is also the god of the sky and law.

Eleggua/Legba – Eleggua is the god of the crossroads and fate. He is associated with black, red and the number 3. Legba is a trickster god, a messenger and the god of fate. He also rules the crossroads.

Shangó/Chango – Both are gods of thunder and lightning. Shangó is also connected with justice, dancing and drumming. He is associated with the ram's head, red, white and the number 4. Chango is also a warrior god who protects land and wealth.

Yemayá/Yemonja – Both are mother goddesses and the goddesses of the ocean and water. Both goddesses are associated with cowrie shells. In Santeria, she is associated with blue and the number 7. In Vodun, she is connected to the moon.

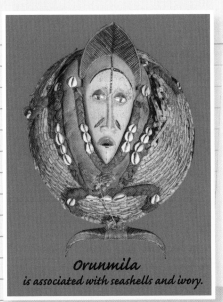

Orunmila
is associated with seashells and ivory.

A Santerian cast-iron spellpot found in a cemetery.

Ogún/Ogun – *Ogún is the god of iron and war. He is associated with green, black and the number 7. Ogun is the god of iron and steel. He is also associated with growing crops and hunting.*

Oshún/Oshun –*Oshún is the goddess of beauty, sensuality, pregnancy and rivers. She is associated with yellow and the number 5. Oshun is the goddess of love, art and sensuality. Both goddesses are primarily honoured by women, but are also connected to healing.*

Oyá/Orunmila – *Oyá is the seventh major deity in Santeria, but only a minor deity in Vodun. In Santeria, Oyá is the goddess of storms who lives at the cemetery gates. She is associated with red, yellow, blue and the number 9. Orunmila is the seventh major Vodun deity. He is the god of wisdom, destiny, divination and healing.*

How the African Gods Travelled West
African slaves were predominantly taken from the Ashanti, Dahomey and Yoruban tribes of West Africa. The Dahomeans and Yorubans were largely sent to Spanish lands, where they were forcibly converted to Catholicism. The Ashantis were mostly sent to English lands, where the slaveholders saw no need to convert them. Vodun emerged in Haiti, and Santeria in Cuba and Puerto Rico. Both faiths mingle the African gods with the Catholic saints.

Tribal Masks
Symbolic masks are worn by dancers during religious ceremonies to help them communicate with the gods.

HINDU ÐEITIES

The Hindu gods have been worshipped for thousands of years. Hindu mythology is quite extensive and convoluted, consisting of millions of deities with hundreds of names. Most modern Witches choose to work with a few primary gods, usually drawn from the 33 listed in the Vedas. The Vedas are sacred Hindu texts composed around 1000 BCE, but not written down until nearly 2,500 years later.

The Brahman, Devas and Murtis

The Brahman is the supreme Hindu deity. Ultimately, everything in the universe descends from and is an aspect of the Brahman. The other primary Hindu deities are the murtis and devas/devis. The murtis are avatars (incarnations) of the Brahman. The devas (gods) and devis (goddesses) are forms of the Brahman, but also deities in their own right. They typically represent aspects of the world or of life. Many of them have dual roles or multiple associations due to the Hindu focus on balance.

The Trimurti

Three gods are considered the most important after the Brahman.

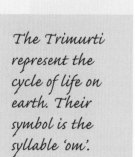

Brahma the creator, who was himself created by the Brahman, is a god of knowledge and prosperity. He carries the Vedas in his hands. His wife is Sarasvati. Brahma is usually depicted with four heads facing the four directions and is associated with the goose.

Vishnu the protector maintains the balance between good and evil in the universe. He has had nine incarnations, or avatars. Krishna was his eighth avatar and Buddha was his ninth. The tenth has not yet arrived. His wife is Lakshmi. He is also a god of love and of the sun.

Shiva the destroyer, who is also the god of sex, is represented by the phallus and the boar. His wife is Parvati. Shiva is often depicted in meditation, or as the lord of the dance, dancing upon the demon of ignorance.

The Trimurti represent the cycle of life on earth. Their symbol is the syllable 'om'.

shiva

Shakti and the Tridevi

Shakti is the supreme mother goddess; the universe rests in her womb. In some forms of Hinduism, Shakti is worshipped as the supreme deity, while in others she represents the creative energy of the Brahman and the female counterpart of the male gods. The three goddesses of the Tridevi – Sarasvati, Lakshmi and Parvati – are the wives of the Trimurti gods and also their female shaktis (or avatars).

Sarasvati, the goddess of wisdom and the arts, is the wife of the creator Brahma, which makes her a mother goddess. She is associated with fertility and harvests. She may have originated as a river goddess, and is therefore associated with powerful water. She is also connected to prosperity and is a protector of students.

Lakshmi is an earth goddess and a wife of Vishnu. She is also a goddess of prosperity and good fortune. She grants appeals for children, health and success. She is associated with good fishing and good crops; the elephant and the cow are among her symbols. She is worshipped at home rather than in temples.

Parvati is a mother goddess and the wife of Shiva. Together, they represent the sexual union of male and female. Parvati is sometimes regarded as the supreme representation of Shakti.

Other Prominent Hindu Deities

Ganesha

Krishna, the eighth avatar of Vishnu, was sent to earth to rid the world of demons. He is a prankster god, but also a protector. He is the god of love and erotic pleasure. He is also associated with plants.

Varuna keeps the heavenly bodies in place and maintains the system of winds and sea on earth. He represents destiny and truth, and is associated with the horse.

Ganesha is an elephant-headed god created by Parvati. He is a god of prosperity, wisdom and art, as well as wise action. He is called upon to help people overcome obstacles, open a business or travel. He also guards the household.

Kali is a destroyer goddess, but also connected with rebirth. She is black and has four arms, in which she carries the symbols of life and death. She wears a necklace of skulls and a belt of severed limbs. She was sent to earth to battle demons, but her bloodlust continued until she killed Shiva.

Durga is a warrior goddess and a death goddess with multiple arms, each holding a weapon. She is also a great beauty, and is associated with lions and tigers. She is a goddess of the fertility of the land, and is sometimes revered as a goddess of the family.

Kali

Durga

CHAPTER TWO

Magical and Divinatory Tools

Magical and divinatory tools are used to support your magical work. The physical tools help you to focus your magical energy. The divinatory tools offer guidance about the correct course of action, or provide insight into your life and current state of mind. In addition to the magical and divinatory tools described here, you may find additional items or divination methods that are useful to you. There is no right or wrong way to incorporate them into your practice.

TYPES OF TOOLS

Witches use several tools in the course of their magical practice. No tool is essential, though, and any spell can be performed with only your mind and your words. If you do choose to use tools, take your time gathering them. It is better to work without a tool than to rush out and collect them all at once. You will know when you find the right tools for your practice.

Major Tools

Witches rely on a few primary tools when performing magic:
- Candles
- Athame (dagger)
- Chalice
- Cauldron
- Wand
- Broom

Why Use Tools?

Although tools are optional, they are very helpful to a beginning Witch. Using them reminds you that you are in another realm. Until you are practised in the art of magic, they help you to focus and direct your energy. It is easier to visualize energy extending from the point of an athame than from the tip of a finger, but in actuality, the finger is just as effective.

The tools also connect us to our traditions. Although Wicca is less than 100 years old, some of the tools and traditions are drawn from much older faiths. Tools connect us not only to the pre-Christian traditions we suspect were practised by our ancestors, but also to the traditions that have developed in the faith over the last 80 years.

Some common Witch's tools.

Always clean your tools after use.

Shared Tools

If you have a coven or working circle, you can share some of your tools with them. Some Witches keep two sets of tools – one for personal use and one for group use. Others simply trust that their covenmates will recognize the importance of treating the tools with respect.

Altar and Attire

- Like all tools, formal altars are optional. If you are not using any other tools, then an altar is unnecessary. If you do choose to use an altar, follow the instructions on pages 76–79 for setting up temporary and permanent altars around your home.

- You do not actually need a robe or any other special clothes to practise magic. Many Witches practise in the nude; working nude helps you to move out of the everyday world, and is good for fire safety when using candles.

The Four Witches by Albrecht Dürer, 1497

Choosing a Robe
If you wish to wear a robe for public or outdoor rituals, look for these qualities:
- Floor length
- Sleeveless or fitted around the wrist (for safety when working with candles)
- Hooded
- Lightweight and light-coloured for spring/summer
- Heavy, warm and dark-coloured for autumn/winter

Divinatory Tools

- Divination is a major component of a Witch's toolset. You can choose from several popular forms, or rely on a more obscure method. The key is to practise it until you become proficient at interpreting the results.

- Witches often use astrology and numerology to determine the influence of outside forces on the past, present and future.

- Many Witches perform divination before casting a spell to confirm that it is the right course of action or that the spell is written correctly. The most popular divination tools for this purpose include tarot, runes and scrying.

CONSECRATING YOUR TOOLS

Before using any tool or object in a ritual or spell, you should cleanse and consecrate it. Once a tool is consecrated, you should only use it for magical purposes. It should also be properly stored and maintained to ensure that its magical energy does not weaken. Should it become clouded with negative energy or be misused, you can recleanse and reconsecrate it.

Tool Storage
Once consecrated, your tools should be stored separately from your common household objects. If you keep an altar, some of your tools can reside on it. If you have room, place a box or closed basket under the altar for the rest of your tools. You can also keep them in their own drawer, shelf or box. If any item, such as a crystal ball or a scrying mirror, might collect negative energy, wrap it in a piece of black silk.

Cleansing Tools

There are several ways to cleanse a tool before its first use. The most common cleansing methods are:

- Set it on a bed of rock salt for three days.
- Leave it overnight in the light of a full moon.
- Wash it with pure spring water or water mixed with sea salt.
- Bury it in the earth for three days.
- Pass it through smoke; traditionally, a feather is used to fan sage smoke over the tool.

Note: The most appropriate method depends on the material the tool is made from. Avoid using salt to cleanse metal objects, and be careful using water with iron tools. Wooden tools may also not respond well to salt. Do not use water with wooden objects unless they are coated with a sealant.

Burying a chalice in the earth will cleanse it for magical use.

Consecration Ritual

After cleansing a tool, you need to consecrate
it on the next new or full moon, before using it
in your spells and rituals. You can consecrate
several tools at once, or each one separately.

You will need:
- Candle, ideally light-coloured
- Sage wand (see page 137)
- Dish of salt water

1 Set up your ritual space, then cast a magic
circle (see page 101) or meditate until
your mind is clear (see page 80).

2 Invoke the goddess and god, saying: 'Great
Mother, Great Father, I ask you both to join me
as I consecrate this [tool] for magical work.'

3 Light the candle and sage, then place your hands
on the tool and say, 'I consecrate this [tool]
for magical purpose. It is released from all
worldly energy and carries the energy of
all the elements.'

4 Pass it over the candle flame, saying, 'By the
fire, it is blessed.' Pass it through the sage
smoke, saying, 'By the air, it is blessed.'
Sprinkle salt water on it, saying, 'By earth
and water, it is blessed.'

5 Place your hands on the tool again and say,
'I consecrate this [tool] for magical purpose.
May it bring me transformation, health and
wisdom. This [tool] is consecrated by all the
elements and by the will of the gods. An' it
harm none, so mote it be.'

6 Thank the goddess and god for joining you
and then release them, saying: 'Farewell
and blessed be.'

7 Let the candle and sage wand burn down.

Sage

Visualize the flame's energy filling the tool with its power.

CANDLES

Candles are one of the Witch's most important tools, and have multiple uses in both rituals and magic. Candles symbolize the element of fire, but can also be associated with the directions, deities or any other number of things. Candles come in all shapes, sizes and colours, and although they are very affordable, it is also easy to make your own. Candle wax and rolls of wick can be found at craft shops or online.

Candles and Deities
Candles can represent the god and goddess in simple spells. The goddess candle is usually green or silver, to honour her association with either the earth or the moon. The god candle is either red or gold, to recognize his association with the sun. The goddess candle should be on the left of the altar, and the god candle on the right.

Making Rolled Candles

1. Lay a sheet of beeswax on a cutting board. Cut the wax to size using a sharp knife and ruler; 10cm (4in) tall candles are perfect for spells.

2. Soften the wax with a hair drier on the warm setting for about 30 seconds.

3. Lay the wick along the height edge of the wax, and press the wax edge over the wick to hold it in place.

4. Roll the candle slowly, evenly and tightly.

You will need:
- Sheet of beeswax
- Wick
- Cutting board that you do not plan to use for food again
- Sharp knife
- Ruler
- Hair drier

Never blow out a candle.

It is considered an insult to the element (fire). Instead, use your fingers or a snuffer to snuff it out.

Making Dipped Candles

1. Cut the blocks of wax into small pieces, keeping the colours separate. If you cannot find coloured wax, shavings of coloured wax crayons will do at a pinch.

2. Heat some water to a gentle boil over a medium heat.

3. Place the second pot of a double boiler or a large can on top. Put the pieces of paraffin wax inside. Melt them over a medium heat, until the wax is about 70°C (160°F). Add the coloured wax a little at a time, and stir until it reaches the desired colour. It will lighten when cool, so test a little on a plate.

4. Cut the wick to the appropriate length. For two 20cm (8in) candles, cut a 50cm (20in) piece.

5. Wrap the centre of the wick around the dowel once.

6. Dip the wick into the wax for a few seconds, then lift out and let it harden. Repeat until it reaches the desired thickness at the base. Do not let the wet candles touch each other.

7. To speed the process after the first few layers, dip the candles in cold water between layers. If they become lumpy, roll them on a flat surface a few times.

8. Increase the wax temperature to 80°C (182°F) and dip one more time.

9. Trim the bottom of the candles with a knife to flatten them.

10. Hang the dowel and allow the wax to dry completely. A clothes-drying rack is great for hanging candles when drying.

You will need:
- Block of plain paraffin wax
- Blocks of wax in the colours of your choice
- Wick
- Sharp knife
- Ruler
- Cutting board
- Double-boiler or a saucepan and large tin can
- Wax or candy thermometer
- Short length of thick dowel

Candles and Colours

Most candle colours have several magical correspondences, but each has a primary meaning:

- **Red:** Love
- **Orange:** Career
- **Yellow:** Persuasion
- **Green:** Prosperity
- **Blue:** Healing
- **Purple:** Spirituality
- **White:** Purity
- **Black:** Protection

Birthday candles are an easy way to add colour to your spells.

Scented Candles

Avoid scented candles unless you are making them yourself with essential oils. Most commercial candles have a strong, chemical-based scent.

AThaME

The athame, or ritual dagger, is the Witch's most common tool after candles. Most Witches seek out an athame before obtaining a wand or cauldron. The athame has a primary role in rituals and spells, although it is not absolutely necessary. It represents the element of fire, although some traditions associate the athame with air. The word is pronounced either ah–THAw-mee or ATH-uh-may.

The Kitchen Witch's Athame

Kitchen Witches practise the magic of the kitchen. Some cook special foods to work their magic, while others see every meal as a part of their practice. If you are a Kitchen Witch, your chef's knife may very well be your athame.

How to Find Your Athame

When looking for an athame, do not buy the first one you see unless it really speaks to you. Instead, keep your eyes open as you visit Pagan, antique, hunting or even stationery shops. When you feel drawn to a blade, hold it in your hand. Test the heft and the grip. Can you feel yourself working with this? Do not worry about the sharpness. Although a knife, the athame is not used for physical cutting.

Excalibur

The Original Athame

Some consider the legendary sword Excalibur to be the original athame. Forged from steel and drawn only by the chosen one, it was the source of King Arthur's power. Following that tradition, some Witches choose to use a sword rather than a smaller blade.

Some Witches decorate their athame with magical symbols.

Traits to Look For

Every athame is unique, and you have a lot of options when looking for the right blade. Although it is also called a black-handled knife, the handle can actually be any colour. Traits commonly found in athames include:

- Dull blade
- Iron blade
- Steel blade
- Stone or crystal blade
- Wood handle
- Stone or crystal handle
- Typically 15cm (6in) long
- Serpentine blade
- Straight blade

Uses for an Athame

The athame has many uses in magic, but none of them is related to physical cutting. That role is reserved for the white-handled knife, or bolline (see page 73). Instead, the athame is used for the following:

- Casting and opening a magic circle.
- Invoking the god and goddess.
- Symbolizing the male in a symbolic Great Rite (see page 66).
- Initiation challenge.
- Directing magical energy.

As with any good kitchen knife, keep your athame sharp and treat it with the care and respect it deserves.

Traits to Avoid

- If you plan to work with the faery folk, avoid steel or iron athames because these metals repel them.
- Always avoid plastic athames; there is nothing magical about plastic.

Athame Searching Charm

If you have trouble locating your first blade, say these words to help guide you to it:

'Lord of light, brighten the path to my athame.

Lead me to my sacred blade.'

The Sickle

Witches who work heavily with herbs, and grow their own as part of their practice, may have a sickle-shaped athame that they use for magic as well as for culling herbs. Others may have a specially blessed sickle for cutting herbs in addition to a primary athame for the spells themselves.

WAND

The wand plays the most prominent role in rituals and spells, after the athame (ritual dagger). Seen in movies and TV shows featuring wizards and magicians, the wand has a true magical purpose as a director of energy. It usually represents the element of air, but may represent fire in some traditions. Some Witches use a large staff instead of a wand, or have both a wand and a staff.

Crystal or Wooden Wands
Witches who work extensively with crystals might have a crystal wand, but wood is more traditional.

Suitable Woods for Wands

Although a wand can be made of nearly any wood, a few woods are considered traditional:
- Apple
- Ash
- Oak
- Holly
- Maple
- Cherry
- Willow
- Hazel

Wand Characteristics

Wands come in all shapes and sizes, but a few characteristics are common to most:

- The length of the wand usually equals the distance from the tip of your fingers to the tip of your elbow.
- It is as straight as possible.
- It is made of wood that has been sanded smooth, with any nubs removed.
- The shape of the wand is tapered slightly at the top.

Gathered at Glastonbury during a new moon.

The Apple Wand
Some people have multiple wands for different kinds of spells. Legend states that love spells are best performed with a wand made from apple wood. If you work with faeries, they prefer apple wands, too.

Making a Wand

**Although you can buy a wand, they are
very simple to make. Homemade wands
also have the most power.**

1. Go for a hike and look for a small fallen
   twig or branch. Pull twigs from an apple or
   willow tree. If you have a garden, look for
   thick vines or rose bushes. You will know
   when you find the right wood. If you cut
   the wood from a tree, visit the tree during
   a full moon, ask permission to cut the twig
   and then thank the tree for its gift.

2. Allow the wood to dry out completely, then use
   a sharp knife to whittle off any buds, twigs or
   nubs. Strip off the bark, and taper the tip
   slightly. Sand the wood smooth.

3. Decorate the wand. If you wish, you can stain
   the wand or add a varnish or lacquer. Many
   people attach crystals to the tips, carve magical
   symbols into the shaft and attach charms or
   feathers. You can also wrap the wand with
   leather. If you are good at woodcarving, you
   could carve the ends into a decorative shape.

4. When the wand is complete, bless and consecrate
   it for use (see pages 58–59).

Decorate your wand with
anything you like – feathers,
colourful leather thongs,
crystals and so on.

Wands have two primary uses

1 Casting and opening a magic circle.
2 Directing energy during magic.

CHALICE

The chalice represents the goddess, fertility and the element of water. Its primary purpose is to hold a libation that will be offered during a magic ritual. It has a secondary role as the representation of the goddess in a symbolic Great Rite. Although the chalice is traditionally a goblet, some Witches use an ale flagon instead.

Great Rite
The consummation of the god and goddess's sacred marriage is known as the Great Rite. Witches sometimes perform a symbolic Great Rite, particularly during fertility spells, which involves dipping the athame (phallus) into the chalice (vagina).

Chalice Well
Chalice Well in Glastonbury, England, is a natural spring that has been reputed to have healing properties since ancient times. It is associated with the goddess, and the legends of King Arthur and the Holy Grail. Visitors today are welcome to take a small amount of water from the well.

Warning: Avoid any chalice that contains lead (which excludes some pewter), or that is not sealed with a food-safe material.

Charged Chalice Water

In healing spells, you can boost the energy by drinking charged chalice water.

1 Light a white candle and fill the chalice with water.

2 Hold the tip of the athame or wand over the chalice.

3 Imagine a stream of white energy coming through your head, then through your hand, and finally out the tip of the wand or athame. This is goddess energy.

4 Say, 'Goddess, bless these waters for healing. Imbue the water with your cleansing energy, that it may wash away all that blocks my health.'

5 Continue with the rest of the spell.

Ceremony of Cakes and Ale

- In formal rituals, it is traditional to complete a spell by performing the ceremony of Cakes and Ale.
- If working outside, sprinkle a bit of both on the ground and say: 'Lady, thank you for your gifts of the earth. Lord, thank you for your gifts of the vine [or tree or field].'
- If you are performing the spell with a partner, offer each other the cakes with the words 'May you never hunger,' and the ale with the words 'May you never thirst.' If performing the spell alone, present them to yourself.

Chalice Materials

A chalice should be watertight, and difficult to break (in case it tumbles over during a spell). When choosing a chalice, it should be made from one of the following materials:

- Clay
- Stone
- Wood
- Metal (for example, bronze, silver or gold)

Types of Cake and Ale

The cakes can be biscuits, cake or even fruit. The ale can be wine, beer, mead or fruit juice. The cakes are a gift from the goddess, and the ale is a gift from the god.

Chalice Decoration

Your chalice can be as simple or ornate as you like. Some Witches choose carved chalices, chalices adorned with crystals or a simple plain wooden goblet.

CAULDRON

A traditional cauldron is not an essential spellcasting tool – any pot will do – but an iron cauldron is a useful addition to any Witch's tool collection. Cauldrons symbolize the element of water, but they are also used to contain fire. Cauldrons appear in ancient lore as fonts of wisdom and sources of sustenance. They retain enormous magical power today.

Cauldron Sizes and Materials
The traditional material is iron, but you can use any fire-resistant metal. Cauldrons range in size from 95-litre (25-gallon) cauldrons for group rituals, to small 8.5 x 12.5cm (3 x 5in) kettles perfect for a personal altar. You can also find 18cm (7in) tall potbelly cauldrons with pentagrams forged on the front.

Chiminea

Legendary Celtic Cauldrons

Celtic lore describes several cauldrons:

- The Cauldron of Plenty was brought to Ireland by the god Daghdha and provides nourishment, enough for an army.
- The Cauldron of Rebirth belongs to the Welsh giant and king, Bran the Blessed. Any warrior who dies in battle can be placed in the cauldron to be reborn, but he will not be able to speak afterwards.
- The Cauldron of Wisdom brings inspiration and divine knowledge. It is sometimes associated with the Holy Grail.
- The silver Gundestrup Cauldron, which dates to the 1st or 2nd century BCE, was found in a peat bog in Denmark. It depicts Celtic gods and warriors, and may show an initiation ritual (see page 41).

Improvising a Cauldron
If you do not have a cauldron, these are good substitutes:
- Iron Dutch oven
- Steel stock or sauce pot (uncoated)
- Unpainted ceramic flowerpot with base
- Small chiminea
- Fire pit
- Barbecue (use outdoors only)
- Large stone mortar
- Iron kettle (not a tea kettle)
- Brazier

Performing Cauldron Spells

- A cauldron can be used in any kind of spell, but it is especially powerful for transformational spells. Transformational spells create change in your life, either by banishing something negative or by manifesting something positive.

- In lieu of a formal spell, you can simply meditate, write down your request to the gods on parchment paper and then burn it. Once the paper is burned away, dispose of the ashes by burying them, or sprinkling them in the garden or into a moving body of water.

- Burn herbs in the cauldron to amplify the magical energy of your spells.

- If you are making a potion in your cauldron, focus all of your magical energy on your goals as you brew the potion.

- Use your cauldron during magical celebrations, such as for apple bobbing during Samhain (Halloween) festivities.

Two Witches brewing a hailstorm in their cauldron.

Caring for Your Cauldron

- Wipe out the cauldron with a damp cloth if ash builds up on the inside.
- If you use it for cooking, follow the usual instructions for cleaning iron or metal cookware.
- Keep the cauldron on or under your altar, or with your other magical tools between uses.
- If it is used by friends for non-magical purposes, or used for a powerful banishing spell, you may want to recleanse and reconsecrate it (see pages 58–59).

Use your cauldron for apple bobbing on Halloween.

BROOM

The image of a Witch soaring on her broom is common around Halloween, but due to the laws of physics, Witches cannot really use brooms to fly – they rely on aeroplanes for that. The broom, also called a besom, does serve a magical purpose, however, and is an important addition to a Witch's tool collection. The broom is used for protection and purification. It need not be large – even a small handheld broom will do for magical work.

Jumping the Broom

This custom, originating from both Wales and Africa, is continued in Wiccan weddings (handfastings) today. Following the ceremony, the couple step over the broom to bless their fertility and their union. The broom is typically decorated with flowers and ribbons, and hung in a prominent place in the couple's home after the wedding.

Origins of the Broom

During the persecutions of the Witch Craze in Europe (c1450–1750), some victims reported applying a flying ointment to their bodies, and then jumping around on brooms. Flying ointment recipes found in the records often contain psychedelic ingredients, but they also often contain poisons, which casts doubt on the truth of these claims.

Broom Uses

A magical broom is not used for actual sweeping. That task falls to regular brooms. Instead, the magical broom is used to sweep out negative energy at the following times/places:

- From corners during a house blessing.
- Before casting a magic circle prior to performing a ritual or spell.
- Out of a person during a cleansing ritual.

Brooms and Protection

According to folklore, a broom hung over or near a doorway with the bristles pointed up will protect the home from negative energy.

Buying a Broom
If you buy a magical broom instead of making one, do not go to the hardware shop to find it. Avoid brooms that are held together with glue or metal, contain plastic or are designed for household use.

Handle Woods
The broom handle can be made from a variety of sturdy branches. The following are the most common:
· *Birch*
· *Hazel*
· *Ash*
· *Oak*

How to Make a Broom

You can find decorative twig brooms in craft and home-decorating shops during autumn, but you can also make your own.

1. Soak the bristle material in water overnight. Let it dry for a few hours until it is supple but not waterlogged.

2. Arrange a layer of bristles around the base of the branch and tie tightly with twine.

3. Add another layer, building outwards until the bristles reach the desired fullness and shape.

4. Add a final layer, with 15cm (6in) of bristle covering the broom handle. Wrap the twine securely around the top layer, 7.5cm (3in) from the base of the handle. Fold the bristles over the twine to hide it. Tie a length of twine tightly near the top of the bundle. Tie a second length about 5cm (2in) down.

5. If you wish, decorate the handle or the top of the bristle bundle with crystals, paint or carvings.

Bristle Materials
· *Straw*
· *Wheat*
· *Twigs, such as willow*
· *Lavender*
· *Mugwort*
· *Thyme*

MINOR TOOLS

In addition to the major tools, Witches use a variety of minor tools for different kinds of spells. As always, none of the tools is absolutely essential, and other tools can be substituted. However, as you grow in the Craft, you may wish to add a few of these items to your permanent collection.

Draw a pentagram in one go, starting from the top point down to the lower left point.

Pentacle

A pentagram is a five-pointed star; a pentacle is a pentagram with a circle around it. Many Wiccans wear pentacle jewellery as a symbol of their faith. The pentacle also has a role in magic. During a spell, place your spell materials, like crystals or candles, on top of the pentacle to boost the magical energy.

A pentacle can be made of clay, metal, wood or even paper, and embellished with magical symbols.

Symbolism of the Pentacle

The five points of the pentacle symbolize the elements of earth, air, fire, water and spirit. The pentacle is typically drawn with a single point up, but reversed (upside-down) pentacles are also used. In Wicca, a reversed pentacle demonstrates that the wearer has reached the second of three levels of initiation. It does not have any negative or black magic connotations.

The Bell

When casting a magic circle for spellwork, some Witches ring a bell to announce that they are about to enter the other realm. They ring the bell again at the end of the spell to open the circle and signal the return to the mundane world. Some Witches use the bell to help them enter meditation. Others believe that the sound of a bell wards off negative spirits.

White-Handled Knife

Also called a bolline (BOW-leen), the white-handled knife is a Witch's primary working knife. The handle can actually be any colour and material, but it should be a sharp, straight blade. Once it has been consecrated for magical use, do not use it for common household tasks. Only use your bolline for cutting herbs, carving symbols into candles and cutting cords during a spell.

Making a knife
It is possible to make a beautiful magical knife yourself from an old blade and a piece of wood or bone for the hilt.

Keep the blade sharp.

Parchment Paper

Spells are traditionally written on parchment paper. Although originally made from sheepskin, non-animal parchment paper can now be found at good stationery shops. It does not burn quite as well as sheepskin parchment, but does burn more cleanly than regular paper; regular paper will do at a pinch, though. Be very careful when burning parchment; it ignites quickly. Follow these steps to ensure fire safety:

1 Cut a small square before the spell. If you need a large piece, fold it into a smaller square before lighting.
2 After meditating, dip the corner of the parchment into the candle flame.
3 Immediately drop it into a cauldron or cauldron substitute.
4 If the paper will not tuck fully inside or falls out, use your white-handled knife to poke it into the cauldron.
5 If the spell calls for it, toss herbs on top of the paper. Never place a candle or any other kind of wax inside the cauldron.
6 Allow the container to cool before attempting to move it.

Parchment sample; burns well.

Using parchment
Writing a spell on parchment helps you to focus on your goal, which encourages the spell to come true.

UnuSuaL ItemS

Many spell books require tools or ingredients that are difficult to find, such as lodestones and witch bottles. Although these objects are nice to have, it is usually easier and just as effective to substitute a common household object. Here are a few of the typical tools and ingredients that can be replaced with items you already have at home.

Witch Bottle
A witch bottle is traditionally a round glass bottle with a stopper that is used for protection. If you cannot find one, use any glass jar with a stopper or lid. Even a wine bottle will do. Put any of the following items inside it:
• Nails or needles
• Skeleton keys
• Dried garlic
• Frankincense
• Pepper
• Pine needles
• Black onyx or obsidian chips
• Sea salt
• Vinegar
Once filled, seal the lid with black candle wax, consecrate it and then hide it somewhere in your home.

Hawk Feather
Some spells call for special feathers, like hawk or eagle, that may be difficult to find or even illegal to own – in the United States, it is illegal for non-Native Americans to possess the feathers of prey birds. If you cannot find or cannot own a specific type of feather called for in a spell, any other feather will do. You can often find ostrich or peacock feathers in craft shops.

Witch Ball
A witch ball is a gold, green or blue glass sphere that villagers hung in their windows to ward off evil spirits. You can use a thick glass Christmas ornament instead. In fact, Christmas ornaments originated as witch balls.

Lodestone
A lodestone is a piece of magnetite, and is attracted to magnetic fields. If you cannot find magnetite or a lodestone, a plain household magnet is a suitable substitute. Before using it, cleanse it in a bowl of rock salt or leave it out in the light of a full moon overnight.

Dragon's Blood Ink

If a spell calls for dragon's blood ink and a quill pen, you can go to a New Age shop in search of them, or you can simply use a regular red ink pen. The true ink is produced from a red resin.

Seed Pod Rattle

A seed pod rattle is a small seed pod dried on a long stem. The seeds inside are loosened by the drying process. You can often find these in the shops of natural history museums, or make your own by plucking a large seed pod from your garden or a nearby field and hanging it to dry. If you cannot find a seed pod rattle, a dried gourd with interior seeds or a small wooden rattle will do instead. Visit New Age shops, museum shops or drum shops for rattles of all kinds.

Cemetery Dirt

Some spells call for cemetery dirt, because it is hallowed ground and may harbour the energy of spirits. If you do not want to visit a cemetery to collect dirt, consecrate soil from your own garden. Spirits residing in cemeteries are unsettled, so they may not contribute the ideal energy to your spell anyway.

Skeleton Key

Skeleton keys are old-fashioned keys that can fit multiple locks. You can often find them affordably at antique shops, but you could also visit a hardware shop and ask for a key blank. You might already have a skeleton key if you have dining room hutches or secretaries with decorative locks and keys.

Poppet

A poppet is a small doll used to represent another person or yourself in spells. Poppets are traditionally used for curses, but can also be helpful for healing or binding spells. If you cannot find a small cloth doll, a small teddy bear will do at a pinch. You can also make a poppet by following these directions:

1 Buy remnant fabric and cotton stuffing.
2 Fold the fabric in half and cut it out in the shape of a person (a gingerbread man shape will do).
3 With right sides together, stitch around the edges, leaving a hole at the top.
4 Turn inside out.
5 Stuff the poppet loosely.
6 Stitch the top closed.

ALTARS

Altars come in several shapes and forms, and can be permanent or temporary. They can serve as a general altar for all magical work, be dedicated to a deity or person, or be focused around a specific life area. Altars can be the size of a table, or just a small shelf tucked into a corner of your home. Whatever sort of altar you choose to make, it is important that you maintain it carefully and treat it with respect.

Suitable Altars

The following items can serve as an altar:
- Wooden stool or table.
- Top of a dresser.
- Shelf or wooden plank resting atop small stacks of books or similar.
- Any surface with a small arrangement of symbolic objects on top.

Purpose of Altars

The altar is the place where a Witch performs spells, keeps the remnants of spells and conducts worship.

An altar may be set up to:

- Perform spells and divination.
- Attract something into your life, like love.
- Celebrate a seasonal or lunar ritual.
- Honour the dead, a person or group of people, or a deity or pantheon of deities.

Caring for an Altar

Altars intended for a single spell should be arranged just prior to the spell. Permanent altars must be maintained to retain the correct energy and balance – a dusty or cluttered altar reflects a lack of interest and care. If you create an altar to a deity, make regular offerings to it. If you have an altar for a specific purpose, meditate before it regularly to maintain that energy in your life.

Day of the Dead altar, Mexico.

Altar for the Dead

In some cultures, families set up an altar to the dead after they pass. If you wish to honour the recently passed with an altar, you can set it up shortly after the passing or on Halloween. Choose a small, out-of-the-way space. Decorate it with the person's photograph and objects representing their passions and interests. Write him or her a letter and lay it on the altar. On Halloween, light a candle and leave a small offering of his or her favourite food. The altar can stay up as long as you like.

Positioning an Altar

An altar can be set up anywhere in the home. A temporary spell altar should be located wherever you plan to do the spell. A permanent altar should be set out of the flow of traffic in the home so that it is not disturbed. If you follow feng shui, place a temporary altar in the appropriate location of your home. A permanent altar is best suited to the knowledge area in the northeast, but it can go anywhere you like.

North — Career and work
Northwest — Friends and communication
Northeast — Education and knowledge
West — Children and creativity
East — Health and family
Southwest — Love and marriage
Southeast — Wealth and prosperity
South — Recognition and fame

Feng Shui Positions

Feng shui is an Eastern philosophy that aims to harmonize our environment by marrying the location of activities to the area where energy is most supportive to them. If you follow feng shui, place your altar in the appropriate location of your home.

Lararium fresco in Pompeii, Italy

Lararium

In ancient Rome, each family had a lararium, which was a permanent household altar. There might be one altar either in the foyer or on the hearth, or several throughout the house. It offered protection for the home and its inhabitants.

Outdoor Altars

If you prefer to cast spells outside, you can also maintain an outdoor altar. Although you should not leave easily weathered tools on it, the main altar space can be kept sacred year-round. Use a stone altar instead of wood to prevent damage from the elements. You can also choose to arrange small altars to the four elements in the appropriate corners of your garden – for example, a collection of shells or a water feature in the west (water), wind chimes in the east (air), a sundial in the south (fire) and a clay planter in the north (earth).

Altar Arrangement

A traditional ritual altar faces north, but your altar can actually face any direction. Depending on the purpose, you may choose to have it face the direction appropriate to the subject. For temporary altars, you should be able to walk all the way around them. Permanent altars are usually against a wall. Below is an example of a typical altar arrangement.

Goddess symbol
(eg, green candle)

Stone
(north/earth)

God symbol
(eg, red candle)

Chalice
(west/water)

Altar and/or
spell candle

Wand
(east/air)

Athame
(south/fire)

Pentacle and spell ingredients
(alternatively, place these in centre of altar)

Altar Cloths

Most altars are covered with altar cloths. If you have a permanent altar, you can either choose a cloth that you will always use, or change it with each season. If you have a temporary altar, choose a colour that suits your intended purpose – for example, pink for a love spell or green for a prosperity ritual. The cloths can be formal tablecloths or simple squares of fabric. Choose a washable fabric to make it easier to keep the altar clean; it is a good idea to wash the cloth after a major spell to clear it of magical energy.

The Elements

The elements represent the forces of nature. Each one is associated with a compass point and a magical tool.
North: *Earth & pentacle*
East: *Air & wand*
South: *Fire & athame*
West: *Water & chalice*
Note that a stone is placed in the north of the altar to represent earth; the pentacle is placed with the spell ingredients to boost their power.

Altar Blessing

The first time you erect a permanent altar, you should bless it. If the altar ever becomes blocked with negative energy, perform the blessing again.

1 Place the altar in the desired location. Light a sage wand and waft the smoke through the area to remove any negative energy. Symbolically sweep the area clean with a broom.

2 Cast a circle around the altar (see page 101) and invite the elements.

3 Invite the deities, saying, 'Lady of light, lady of the moon, lady of wisdom. Lord of earth, lord of the sun, lord of knowledge. Please join me in blessing my altar.'

4 Lay down an altar cloth if you are using one, then arrange the tools on top. State what each tool represents as you position it; for example, 'The chalice represents the element of water.'

5 Light a white candle and place it at the centre of the altar. Close your eyes and visualize a white sphere forming around the altar. Say, 'I cleanse and consecrate this altar for my magical purposes. May it provide grounding and correct energy.' When the sphere of energy is strong, open your eyes and say, 'This altar is blessed. May it strengthen my magic always.'

6 Thank and release the deities; release the quarters and open the circle.

You will need:
- Sage wand (see page 137) or incense
- Broom
- Tools and decorations for the altar
- White candle

Inviting the Elements

'Air, element of east.
South, element of fire.
Water, element of west.
Earth, element of north.
Please join me in blessing my ritual altar.'

PREPARING FOR DIVINATION

If you are new to divination, or in a confused state of mind, you should spend a few minutes preparing yourself for the experience. Although you can divine in any state of mind, you will probably have more clarity if your mind is quiet when you start. If you find it helpful, you can also use a divination spell or charm to help focus your mind and find the correct answer.

Divination Journal
Most Witches keep a Book of Shadows, which is a collection of all their magical knowledge, including spells and lore. Some also record the results of divination in it, but others keep a separate divination journal. Whichever you choose, note the date, the question, the symbols or cards that appeared and the final answer you arrived at. Over time, you may notice that certain symbols or cards appear repeatedly, which could indicate a major issue or quality you need to explore.

Meditating to Quieten the Mind

If you are too focused on yourself and your surroundings, you may see the answer you want to see rather than the correct answer. Follow these steps to let your unconscious, intuitive mind come forwards before divination:

Lay out the cloth if you are using one and place the tool on top. Light a candle or incense. Close your eyes and breathe slowly.

Count your breaths from 1 to 10, then repeat until your mind is still. Let any thoughts drift by. If you become distracted, start counting from 1 again.

Continue until you can count from 1 to 10 a few times without becoming distracted. You are now ready to start.

Divination Spell

**Use this spell for major questions,
or just to help yourself get into
the proper state of mind.**

1 Lay out the divinatory tool on
   a cloth or altar, then cast a circle
   and call the quarters (see page 101).

2 Invite the goddess and god to join you,
   saying: 'Lady of light and wisdom, lord of
   knowledge and insight, illuminate the path
   for me. Guide me to the answers I seek.
   Let your insights be mine.'

3 Hold the tool in your hand. Close your
   eyes. Imagine white light surrounding
   the tool and infusing it with pure energy.
   Say: 'This tool is blessed with correct insight.'

4 Form the question you wish to be answered in your mind or
   say it aloud. Open your eyes and perform the divination ritual
   appropriate for the tool you are using – for example, lay out
   a spread of tarot cards or
   runes. Open your mind and
   find the answer conveyed by
   your chosen tool.

5 When the divination is complete,
   thank the deities, saying: 'Lady of
   wisdom, lord of knowledge, thank
   you for providing the answer I
   sought. Farewell and blessed be.'

6 Release the quarters and open
   the circle.

Finding an Answer
*With tools such as runes, your
conscious mind holds the
knowledge of the symbols that
your unconscious mind will
interpret. With scrying, let
your unconscious mind lead.*

Divination Charm

If you do not want to do a
full spell, but feel a
charm is necessary,
repeat these words:

'Open my vision, clear my
sight, bring the answer
into the light.'

TAROT

The tarot first appeared in Italy in the 14th century, and was called the tarocco. Today, it is used by Witches and lay people alike for divination. Most Witches use it to reflect the state of mind and issues surrounding the questioner instead of to foretell specific events. It is also used to determine whether a spell or some other action is the correct thing to do and will have the desired outcome.

The Tarot Deck

The tarot is a deck of 78 cards, comprising 22 major arcana cards and 56 minor arcana cards. They can be used together or separately, and each card has a unique meaning.

Choosing a Deck

- There are many different designs of tarot deck. The basic Rider-Waite is considered the learner's deck, because some have the meanings printed on the cards; the symbolism is the easiest to read and the cards include the standard symbols and interpretations.

- Before choosing your first deck, study as many of the cards as you can. Make sure that you can comfortably shuffle and deal the cards. If your local bookshop does not let you touch the cards, visit a New Age shop that has open decks or look for the deck online.

- Many Witches have several decks of various designs. You may wish to have one deck for personal divination and another deck for giving readings to other people.

How to Care for Your Deck

- When not in use, store your deck in its box or in a special tarot bag or box. Some Witches wrap the deck in black fabric to protect it from outside energy.
- If you begin to have trouble working with a deck, cleanse it with sage smoke. If the deck is too associated with negativity to work with it, burn it.
- If you become bored with the deck, give it away to a friend who is interested in learning more about the tarot.

Performing a Tarot Reading

1 After performing the necessary preparations for divination (see pages 80–81), shuffle the cards yourself, or get the person asking the question to do so and then hand the deck back to you.

2 Lay out the cards in the spread of your choice – a spread is a pattern formed by a number of cards. There are numerous tarot spreads; three are described below. The cards should be dealt face down. Some Witches lay them on a piece of black silk, but you can choose any cloth that you feel particularly drawn to.

3 Flip the cards over and interpret them (see pages 84–85).

Reversed Cards
Some Witches read reversed (upside-down) cards as if they are the opposite of the usual meaning. If you do this, flip the cards over from left to right, not top to bottom.

Quick Tarot Spreads

One-card Spread
Select a single card for a quick answer to a simple question.

Three-card Spread
Lay out three cards in a row, starting from the left. From left to right, the cards represent past, present and future, or mind, body and spirit.

Celtic Cross Spread

5 Possible goal or destiny

10 Final outcome

1

2 Immediate influences

Present position

4 Past influences

6 Future influences

9 Hopes and ideals

8 Family and friends

3 Recent influences

7 Negative feelings

Major Arcana

The 22 cards of the major arcana are numbered 0 through 21, with each representing an archetype.

0 The Fool
Important choice requires wisdom and courage.

1 The Magician
Beginning of an important new life cycle.

2 The High Priestess
Intuition and wise judgement; thirst for learning.

3 The Empress
Emotional and material abundance; domestic stability.

4 The Emperor
Wealth and authority; reason dominating emotion.

5 The Hierophant
Kindness and mercy; spiritual leader or adviser.

6 The Lovers
Love, beauty and harmony; loving relationship begins.

7 The Chariot
Stressful problems requiring patience and endurance.

8 Strength
Triumph of positive forces over negative.

9 The Hermit
Beneficial meeting with a wise person.

10 The Wheel of Fortune
Destiny involving great gain or loss; unexpected events.

11 Justice
Balanced judgement and control; fair outcome.

12 The Hanged Man
A willing sacrifice entailing hardship; transformation.

13 Death
Death of the old life brings rebirth of the soul.

14 Temperance
Moderation and
self-control;
harmony.

15 The Devil
Power used
negatively; weird
experience.

16 The Tower
Disruption and
unexpected
events; temporary
setback.

17 The Star
Hope, love,
encouragement
and rebirth;
fulfilment.

18 The Moon
Hidden forces
and deception;
emotional crisis.

19 The Sun
Success,
happiness,
satisfaction and
contentment.

20 Judgement
New lease of
life; rewards for
past efforts.

21 The World
Triumphant
completion;
perfect result.

Minor Arcana

**The 56 cards of the minor
arcana are arranged in four
suits, numbered Ace to Ten,
then Page, Knight, Queen
and King.**

Variations Between Tarot Decks
Different names may be used in some tarot decks –
for example, the Hierophant may be called the Pope,
or the Page may be called the Knave. Strength and
Justice sometimes switch places. The suit of Wands
may be called Clubs or Staves, while Coins may be
called Pentacles. Whatever the name or order of the
cards, however, the meanings remain the same.

The Meaning of the Suits
All of the cards within each
suit deal with a particular
theme. The cards can be
seen as a progression from
the lowest to the highest,
or from the greatest
struggle to the greatest
success. Although Aces are
ones, they are considered
the essence of the suit,
the pure spirit.

Swords
• Air
• Knowledge
• Intellect

Wands
• Fire
• The will

Cups
• Water
• Love
• Emotions

Coins
• Earth
• Prosperity
• Material goods

RUNES

Runes are a set of Norse symbols believed to have been created before 200 BCE. The runes are usually inscribed or painted onto small stones or discs, and then laid out in a pattern known as a spread. The combined symbols are studied to determine the meaning of the spread. Runes are not usually read to predict the future, but rather to determine an issue and a correct course of action to resolve it. The runes are also used in spells cast by Asatruar (Norse Pagans).

Rune Legend

According to Norse legend, the god Odin hung upside down from Yggdrasil, the great World Tree, for nine days and nights in order to receive the runes, which he gave to the people as a gift.

You will need:

- Rune material, such as wood or clay, or stones of roughly uniform size and shape
- Knife, bradawl, paint, drill or blowtorch to inscribe or paint symbols

Making Runes

You can buy a set of runes that come with a book, or visit a New Age shop to find a set. However, it is also easy to make your own.

1 If using wood or clay, carve or shape it into small discs. If using stones, polish them.

2 Inscribe or paint the symbols onto the discs. Use whichever method will leave distinct marks and allow you the most precision. Combine methods, such as a knife and paint, if it feels appropriate. Be careful when using sharp tools.

3 Whatever your chosen method, concentrate on each rune as you craft it. Draw the symbol carefully, focusing on the meaning of the rune in order to imbue it with that energy.

4 Cleanse and consecrate the runes as you would any other tool (see pages 58–59).

5 When complete, keep the runes in a silk or velvet drawstring bag and treat them with respect.

Reading the Runes

Runes can be cast in a variety of patterns. Start with a three-rune spread, representing (from bottom to top) past, present and future. You can also select a single rune to give a quick overview or response to a current situation.

The Rune Set

The modern rune set consists of 24 symbols. The symbols are divided into three sets of eight. The first is associated with the deities Frey and Freya, the second Heimdall and the third Tyr.

 1 Fehu
Prosperity

 9 Hagalaz
Transformation

17 Tiwaz
Intellect

 2 Uruz
Health

10 Nauthiz
Resistance

18 Berkano
Growth

3 Thurisaz
Opposition

 11 Isa
Constraint

19 Ehwaz
Work

 4 Ansuz
Inspiration

12 Jera
Rewards

20 Mannaz
State of mind

 5 Raidho
Travel or journey

13 Eihwaz
Unknown influences

 21 Laguz
Balance

 6 Kenaz
Creativity

14 Perthro
Joy

22 Ingwaz
Contemplation

 7 Gebo
Gifts

15 Algiz
Oversight

23 Othala
Family

  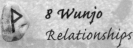 **8 Wunjo**
Relationships

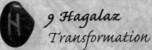   **16 Sowilo**
Guidance

24 Dagaz
Synchronicity

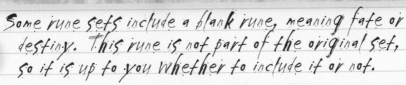
Some rune sets include a blank rune, meaning fate or destiny. This rune is not part of the original set, so it is up to you whether to include it or not.

SCRYING

If you have ever seen a fortune-teller use a crystal ball, then you have seen someone scry, or at least claim to scry. Scrying could be considered a simple form of divination, in the sense that it does not require much equipment or memorization. However, it is really the most difficult, because it involves learning to quieten the mind and see the messages the gods have for us.

Clear quartz balls are traditional, but gla[ss] spheres are commonly used today.

Scrying Tools

- **Crystal balls** are used by most sham fortune-tellers, but they can also be used by legitimate scryers. When using the ball, light a candle in a dark room and gaze into it. Images will form in your mind, not in the ball. Note them for later analysis.

- **Scrying mirrors** are traditionally black and concave. They are rested flat on the table. Some scryers set a candle on top of the mirror, while others set a candle on either side to illuminate the mirror without reflecting the flames. Although your eyes will be focused on the mirror, the images will form in your mind.

- **Incense smoke or a flame** can be used if you do not have a ball or mirror handy. Watch the smoke or flame for symbols or shapes that give some clue as to the answer to your question.

Scrying is best performed at night, especially during a full or new moon. However, you can scry at other times if the need arises.

Herbs for Scrying

The following herbs can be burned as incense to assist you in achieving a receptive state or trance:
- Mugwort
- Wormwood
- Parsley
- Sage
- Thyme
- Rosemary
- Frankincense

Dried Roman Wormwood

How to Make a Scrying Mirror

Rather than buying a scrying mirror, you can make your own very easily.

1 Clean the glass, then use coloured paint to draw magical symbols around the edges on the back of it. Choose symbols that have importance to you. When the symbols are dry, paint over the whole back of the glass with black paint.

2 Mix the dried mugwort and wormwood into half the remaining paint and paint the back of the glass again. When the paint is dry, paint the back one more time with the herb-free paint.

3 Lay the scrying mirror in the light of the full moon overnight, then consecrate the mirror as you do your other tools (see pages 58–59).

4 Keep the mirror wrapped in black silk and out of the light when not in use. Only bring it out when you need to scry.

How to Scry

Meditate to quieten your mind. Say a divination charm (see page 81) and ask a question. Gaze into the mirror, ball, flame or smoke. Let your vision drift so that your mind's eye is dominant. Note any observations on a notepad and let them drift away. Do not force or decide what you are seeing; just let the images come and go. When you do not see anything else, return to your conscious mind to interpret the images you noted.

ASTROLOGY

Astrology is the ancient practice of studying the position and movement of the sun, moon, planets and stars. This information is used to help understand personality traits and predict future events. There are many different schools of astrology, but the three primarily in use today are Western, Vedic and Chinese. Western and Vedic astrology both use the 12 signs of the zodiac; Chinese astrology uses 12 animal signs.

An astrolabe for predicting the positions of the heavenly bodies.

Tropical and Sidereal Zodiacs

The dates associated with the zodiac signs were fixed 3,000 years ago. However, the equinoxes have shifted since that time, so the planets no longer fall on those signs between the assigned dates. The change in dates led to the rise of the Sidereal zodiac, which uses the actual dates the sun rests in a constellation instead of the fixed calendrical dates. The fixed system is known as the Tropical zodiac. Most Western astrologers use the Tropical zodiac; Vedic astrology uses the Sidereal zodiac.

The Signs of the Zodiac

- The zodiac consists of 12 signs based on the 12 constellations of stars through which the sun, moon and planets rotate throughout the year. Each sign lasts approximately 30 days, starting with Aries on the spring equinox (an equinox occurs when the sun is located vertically above a point on the equator, which happens once in spring and once in the autumn).

- Due to the yearly variations in the date of spring equinox, the signs begin and end on slightly different dates each year, but it is always between the 20th and 24th. Those born in that transition period are said to be on the cusp. Although someone born on the cusp may be officially born under one sign, they may also have some characteristics of the adjacent sign.

Some of the zodiac constellations, or groups of stars, in the night sky.

Astrological Horoscopes

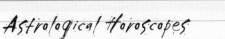

Natal chart

- In Western and Vedic astrology, a horoscope is a chart of the positions of the celestial bodies at a particular point in time. A natal chart is a horoscope based on a person's moment of birth. Astrologers believe that the position of each planet has some effect on your overall personality, body type and health.

- The chart is divided into 12 segments, called houses, that each rule some aspect of life. The planets and zodiac signs rotate through the houses throughout your life. Astrologers believe that the planets have an effect on the houses as they move through them.

- Your sun sign (often referred to as star sign) is in the first house, and then signs progress through the houses of the chart in order. The placement of the planets is determined by consulting an ephemeris, which lists the times and dates each planet rested in a sign.

- Each year, the planets change position in your chart. The chart for each year of your life after birth is called the transit chart, and shows the influences that will most affect your life that year.

The Twelve Houses
The 12 houses of an astrological chart and their associations are:

1 = Ego, self, body
2 = Money, possessions
3 = Communication, siblings, education
4 = Mother, home, family
5 = Pleasure, leisure, creativity
6 = Work, health, diet
7 = Relationships, marriage, all partnerships
8 = Sex, investment
9 = Travel, religion, ideals
10 = Ambition, career
11 = Friends, acquaintances
12 = The occult, seclusion

Saturn Return
Saturn takes nearly 30 years to rotate through your astrological chart, so it will return to its starting point sometime between the ages of 27 and 30, again from 57 to 60 and finally around age 90. The Saturn return marks a period when people confront their fears and doubts. Often, they respond by changing careers, moving, getting married or divorced, or having children.

Western Astrology

The 12 zodiac signs are symbolized by a figure from ancient mythology. This figure represents some aspect of a person born under that zodiac sign, or the constellation's basic character.

Aries
21 Mar–20 Apr
Assertive, urgent,
leader

Taurus
21 Apr–21 May
Steadfast, possessive,
trustworthy

Gemini
22 May–23 Jun
Adaptable, versatile,
communicative

Cancer
24 Jun–22 Jul
Sensitive, caring,
protective

Leo
23 Jul–22 Aug
Creative, dramatic,
powerful

Virgo
23 Aug–22 Sep
Attentive, critical,
analytical

Libra
23 Sep–22 Oct
Thoughtful, diplomatic,
harmonious

Scorpio
23 Oct–22 Nov
Passionate, intense,
purposeful

Sagittarius
23 Nov–22 Dec
Freedom-loving,
inquisitive, adaptable

Capricorn
23 Dec–22 Jan
Prudent, reliable,
persevering

Aquarius
23 Jan–21 Feb
Independent,
inventive, unusual

Pisces
22 Feb–20 Mar
Compassionate,
intuitive, sensitive

Note: The dates given here refer to the fixed Tropical zodiac (see page 90).

Chinese Astrology

The 12 animal signs rotate in a regular cycle, and each governs a year, month and time of day. Chinese astrologers use your year, month and time of birth to cast a horoscope. Year animals represent your outer personality; month animals your relationships; and hour animals your inner nature.

Chinese Calendar

The years given here for each animal refer to their current cycle. Simply add multiples of 12 to your year of birth until you match one of the animals. However, this is just a quick guide. Chinese astrological years are based on the lunar cycle, and the Chinese New Year can fall on any day from late January to late February in the Western calendar. So, if you were born during those months, you need to check the precise date of the New Year to discover your year animal; this information is widely available on the internet.

Rat

2008; December;
11 pm–1 am
Intelligent and
practical

Ox

2009; January;
1 am–3 am
Reliable and
purposeful

Tiger

2010; February;
3 am–5 am
Daring and
passionate

Rabbit

2011; March;
5 am–7 am
Intuitive and
sensitive

Dragon

2012; April;
7 am–9 am
Successful and
independent

Snake

2013; May;
9 am–11 am
Mysterious and
sophisticated

Horse

2014; June;
11 am–1 pm
Hardworking
and friendly

Goat

2015; July;
1 pm–3 pm
Sexy and
adaptable

Monkey

2016; August;
3 pm–5 pm
Quick-witted and
entertaining

Rooster

2017; September;
5 pm–7 pm
Protective and
honest

Dog

2018; October;
7 pm–9 pm
Loyal and
trustworthy

Pig

2019; November;
9 pm–11 pm
Sensual and
eager

NUMEROLOGY

Numerology is the practice of using numbers as a key to understanding a person's lifelong characteristics. Name and birth numbers are the most important. There are several numerological systems; most rely on the numbers 1–9, but some also include the master numbers of 11, 22 and 33. Whatever the system used, your numbers indicate the lessons you are most likely to encounter during your life's journey.

Master Numbers
Some systems consider the numbers 11, 22 and 33 to be master numbers. In those systems, you stop adding the numbers together if you arrive at a master number. In a traditional system, you continue adding, so that the master numbers reduce to 2, 4 and 6.

Name Number

Each letter in the alphabet equates to a number. Write out your name, then write the corresponding number below each letter. Add the numbers together until they reduce to a one-digit number (or stop when you reach a master number).

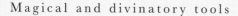

1	2	3	4	5	6	7	8	9
A	B	C	D	E	F	G	H	I
J	K	L	M	N	O	P	Q	R
S	T	U	V	W	X	Y	Z	

Number/Letter Chart
When determining your name number, match the letters with these numbers.

For example:
Selene Silverwind
153555 193459595 4

Add the numbers across = 78
Add the numbers across again = 15
Add the numbers one last time = 6
So the name number for Selene Silverwind = 6

Your life path is determined by your full name as given to you at birth; however, it can be interesting to find the number for the name you have chosen, including your decision to use or not use your middle name or middle initial, any nicknames you prefer to your given name or any name changes.

Birth Number

In addition to your name number, your birth number is very important; unlike your name number, it will never change. There are, however, two ways to determine your birth number. One system stacks the numbers atop each other, adds them and then adds the resulting number across. The other system adds all of the numbers across. In most instances, the final number will be the same, but the intermediate two-digit number could be different. If you work with master numbers, this is an important difference.

Year Number
In addition to determining your birth number, which indicates the lesson you will be working on throughout your life, you can also add the month and day of your birth to the current year to determine the lesson you are currently working on.

For example:
Birthdate 19 October 1971

System 1:

$19 +$
$10 +$
1971
$\overline{2000} = 20 = 2$

System 2:

$1+9+1+0+1+9+7+1$
$= 29 = 11 = 2$

The Meaning of the Numbers
Each of the numbers is associated with a set of personality traits. For example, leaders are often 1s, while artists are often 2s.

1	Leader, ambitious, explorer
2	Imaginative, emotional, adaptable
3	Scientific, not materialistic, curious
4	Eccentric, intuitive, psychic
5	Active, organized, learned
6	Gentle, friendly, peacemaker
7	Psychic, mysterious, generous
8	Pessimistic, successful, hardworking
9	Emotional, jealous, loyal
11	Inspiring, enlightened, inventive
22	Powerful, very successful, idealistic
33	Spiritual leader, teacher, inspiring

Magical Numbers
Name numbers and birth numbers do not typically match, so some Witches choose to take a magical name with a number that corresponds to their birth number.

Christian scholars used numerology to find new meanings in the Bible.

CHAPTER THREE

Spells, Charms and Potions

Once you understand the basic building blocks of a spell, you can do magic in a flash or in a long ceremony. The simple spells and charms in this chapter can be performed with basic household objects and do not require any special skill or knowledge. They only require your pure intent. Potions are also very simple to put together and call for common ingredients — you will not need to seek out eye of newt to achieve your magical goals.

SPELLWORK

Spellwork can take the form of reciting a quick charm, making and using potions or performing rituals. Spells are used for four basic purposes: blessing, honouring, manifesting and banishing. Your goal will fall within those four categories, no matter what it is. The spells in this chapter offer a framework for a variety of goals, but you should draw in other elements as needed to adapt them to your exact goal.

When to Use Magic
If it is easier to do something without magic, then do it. So, if someone you like has asked you on a date, accept the date instead of performing a love spell. However, if you keep dating toads, perform a love spell to attract the right person. You also have to do your part to ensure the desired outcome – if you cast a job spell, for example, you have to send out your CV.

Types of Spells

Manifesting spells Anything you want to attract into your life calls for a manifesting spell. Most Witches cast a large number of manifesting spells. Manifesting should be performed between the new and full moons.

Banishing spells Banishing is the opposite of manifesting. Use banishing spells to rid your life of something. Banishing rituals are typically performed between the full and new moons. The dark moon, the period directly before the new moon, is especially powerful. It can be difficult to determine whether you should banish an old situation or manifest a new one. If you are not sure, consider the emotional impact. If your emotions are blocking the goal, then banish. If you simply have not been lucky enough to achieve what you want, manifest it. You can also banish blocks, and then manifest your goal.

Blessing spells If you have bought a new home, had a child or simply added a new candle to your altar, then a blessing ritual is in order. Blessings should be performed between the new and full moons, or on either of those end points. For larger items, a formal ritual is appropriate. For a small object, a simple blessing charm is sufficient.

Honouring spells Honouring should be reserved for the gods, the moon, special holidays or the deceased. You can use an honouring ritual to thank the gods for helping you to achieve a goal, or to celebrate the full moon or a holiday. When honouring the deceased, build an altar to them and use it in the honouring ceremony. Use whatever funerary traditions are prominent in your culture. Honouring rituals can be performed at any time of the month.

An altar arrangement for a formal spell ritual.

Charms

A charm can be included within a longer spell, or can be a simple spell by itself. A quick charm can be uttered for a basic goal like finding a parking space, or as a confidence booster before a job interview. It can also be used to reactivate the energy of a full ritual spell that you performed earlier.

Blessing Charm

'Lady of light, please bless this [name].

Endow it with power and positive energy. Blessed be.'

Potions

A potion is simply a tea, lotion or other blend of herbs and oils that can bring about a desired magical effect. Potions can be ingested, applied to the body, applied to candles before burning, mixed with bathwater or added to aromatherapy lamps. When choosing herbs for potions and other magical purposes, make sure that you use food-grade herbs.

Storing Potions

- Loose herb blends and bath salts should be stored in glass jars with tight seals.
- Oil blends should be stored in small dark green, amber or dark blue bottles. You can also place the bottles in the refrigerator to reduce evaporation. Warm the bottle between your hands before using the oils.
- Lotions can be kept in a pump bottle or any other lotion bottle that has been washed.
- If you do not use the entire potion and the ingredients are not suitable for storing, dispose of the potion by pouring it onto the earth or into a body of moving water.

THE MAGIC CIRCLE

It is best to perform spells within a sacred space.

A magic circle has three purposes: to separate you from the mundane world; to hold in magical energy until you are ready to release it; and to protect you from negative energy outside the circle. All spells follow a basic framework, and should be performed during the appropriate moon phases (see page 32).

Some Witches like to mark out a circle with salt or chalk, and place a candle in each of the quarters.

Vishnu

Invoking a Goddess or God?
Although the spells in this book often invoke both a goddess and a god, it is not necessary to call both every time. You can choose to call only one deity, or to call multiple deities of the same gender. Most Witches call on the goddess when invoking only one deity, but there are times when it is appropriate to call a god alone, especially for rituals involving men's issues.

Basic Spell Framework

Most spells follow this basic framework:

1 Create a sacred space. Most Witches do this by casting a magic circle; others simply meditate. Casting a circle is best for beginners.

2 Call the quarters (directions) and their elements (earth, air, fire and water). The elements will protect you and lend their power to your goal.

3 Invoke your chosen deities.

4 State your intention and perform the magical working.

5 Thank the deities for their assistance and release them.

6 Release the quarters and open the circle.

Lakshmi

1 To cast the circle at the beginning of a ritual or spell, stand to the north or east of the altar. If this is not possible (your altar may be against a wall), then simply stand in front of it.

Casting the Circle

4 Repeat, 'I cast the sacred circle. I am between the worlds,' until you have walked a complete circle. Now call the quarters (see below) and complete the ritual or spell.

2 Point your athame, wand or a finger of your dominant hand (the one you write with) towards the earth in front of you.

3 Walk clockwise in a circle, either around or in front of the altar, imagining a sphere of energy forming around, above and below you.

Opening the Circle

Open the circle at the end of the ritual or spell, starting in the same place as before. Draw the energy back into your athame, wand or the finger of your non-dominant hand as you walk anticlockwise around the circle, saying: 'The circle is open, but unbroken. Merry meet, merry part and merry meet again.'

Calling the Quarters

To call the quarters after casting a circle, stand facing outwards in the north or east of the circle. Point your athame, wand or a finger of your dominant hand upwards and say: 'I call thee spirit of the [direction]. Please join me and lend me the power of [element]. Blessed be.' Repeat at each remaining quarter, moving clockwise around the circle, then complete the spell or ritual.

Releasing the Quarters

To release the quarters at the end of the spell or ritual, return to the last quarter you called. Stand facing outwards and point your athame, wand or a finger of your non-dominant hand upwards and say: 'Thank you, spirit of the [direction], for joining me and lending me the power of [element]. Stay if you will, go if you must. Farewell and blessed be.' Repeat at each remaining quarter, moving anticlockwise around the circle, then open the circle.

North — **Earth** *Strength & wisdom*

East — **Air** *Intellect & inspiration*

West — **Water** *Emotions & intuition*

South — **Fire** *Passion & energy*

The Quarters and Their Associations
You can change the directions to suit your geographic location, but the qualities associated with each element remain the same. For example, if you live on the east coast of a country, east may represent water to you, so east would also be associated with the emotions and intuition. The square, circle and triangles are the magical symbols for the elements.

Spell Ingredients

Use this chart as a quick reference guide to help you select items whose magical energy corresponds with your goal, as well as the best day for performing the spell.

Goals	Ambition, career, men's issues	Intuition, women's issues	Education, creativity	Love, partnerships, fertility	Sex, courage, passion
Day	Sunday	Monday	Wednesday	Friday	Tuesday
Planet	Sun	Moon	Mercury	Venus	Mars
Deities	Jupiter, Thor, Cernunnos	Isis, Yemaya, Kuan Yin	Athena, Mercury, Ganesha	Aphrodite, Venus, Hathor, Hera	Ares, Freya, Hathor, Oshun
Zodiac signs	Leo	Cancer	Gemini, Virgo	Taurus, Libra	Aries
Elements	Fire	Water	Air, water	Earth, water	Fire
Colours	Yellow, gold, orange	White, silver, grey	Violet, purple, multicolours	Green, pink, rose, indigo	Red
Stones	Topaz, cat's eye, garnet, ruby	Pearl, moonstone, selenite, clear quartz	Opal, agate, jade	Emerald, topaz, lapis lazuli	Carnelian, red jasper, hematite
Herbs	Camomile, heliotrope, orange, sunflower, marigold, frankincense	Moonwort, willow, bergamot, camphor	Caraway, dill, fennel, lavender, pomegranate, valerian, ash, sandalwood, cinnamon	Acacia, apple, birch, daffodil, mugwort, pennyroyal, thyme, mint, verbena, verbain	Aloe, basil, chilli pepper, coriander, dragon's blood, ginger, pepper, holly, tobacco
Metals	Gold	Silver	Aluminium	Copper	Iron, steel
Body parts	Heart	Breasts, female reproductive organs	Brain, nervous and respiratory systems	Throat, lower back, kidneys, parathyroid	Adrenals, intestines, muscles

Shiva

Stones and colours possess magical properties.

Refer to Chapter 1 (pages 14–53) for more in-depth information about spell ingredients.

Business, wealth, justice	Protection, home, karma, obstacles	Inventiveness, reform, change	Dreams, art, healing	Order, uniting, group ideas	Goals
Thursday	Saturday	None	None	None	Day
Jupiter	Saturn	Uranus	Neptune	Pluto	Planet
Jupiter, Njord, Tyr, Ganesha	Saturn, Tsao Chun, Vishnu	Eleggua, Hecate, Loki	Brighid, Apollo, Orunmila	Lugh, Osiris, Varuna	Deities
Sagittarius	Capricorn	Aquarius	Pisces	Scorpio	Zodiac signs
Air, fire	Water, earth	Air, fire, water	Water	Water	Elements
Deep blue, royal purple	Black, blue	Lavender, white	Iridescent colours	None	Colours
Citrine, yellow sapphire	Sapphire, amethyst	Fire opal, clear quartz, aquamarine	Aquamarine, blue quartz, bloodstone, fluorite	Onyx, jet, obsidian, black quartz, black aventurine	Stones
Anise, ash, cinquefoil, clover, cedar, dandelion, mistletoe, nutmeg, sage, oak, olive	Comfrey, yew, cypress, hemp, hemlock, henbane, mandrake, nightshade, myrrh	Rue, clover, birch, ebony wood, High John the Conqueror root	Lotus, watercress, water lily, seaweed	Wormseed, hawthorn, foxglove, ginger, vanilla, arrowroot, dogwood	Herbs
Tin	Lead	Uranium, white gold	Pewter, platinum	Chrome, plutonium	Metals
Liver, pituitary gland	Teeth, bones, skin	None	None	None	Body parts

Manifesting Spells

Manifesting is the art of bringing something into your life through magic and positive thinking. Almost any spell in which you draw something to yourself can be considered a manifesting spell. Career spells and prosperity spells are both forms of manifestation. This section includes spells that can be used for a goal that might not be included elsewhere in this chapter.

Manifesting Goals
Common goals for manifesting spells include:
• Money/prosperity
• A new job
• Repayment of a debt
• A new house or car
• A parking space
• A holiday
• World peace
• Health or healing
• Love
• Confidence
• A child

The Power of Positive Thinking

The key to making any manifestation work is your own mind. You have to truly believe that your spell will be effective and produce the desired result. There are four keys to maintaining the right mindset:

1 Choose the proper goal. It should be attainable in a reasonable amount of time and not harm anyone.

2 Be confident. If you are not sure that you really deserve or want a particular goal, then a manifesting spell will fail. Be confident in your belief that this is the best thing for you.

3 Be willing to accept the consequences. Sometimes even the best-intentioned spells have an unexpected result. You must be willing to accept any and all results of your spell.

4 Forget it. Do not obsess over the spell after you cast it. Instead, go about your life. You will recognize it when the manifested opportunity or result presents itself.

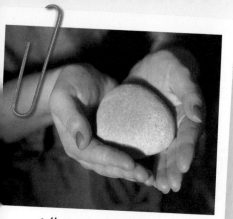

Collect stones while out walking for use in spells.

Manifesting with Stones

Choose the stone or crystal that can help you to manifest a specific goal (see pages 102–103). You can use the stone to assist manifestation in the following ways:

- Bless one for your goal and carry it with you.
- Use one instead of the symbol in the basic manifesting spell (see page 107).

- Use it to clear your chakras of any blocks to your goal (see page 17).
- Place a symbol of the goal on your altar and surround it with related crystals.

Use green stones to manifest fertility.

Manifesting with Herbs

Herbs can be powerful tools for manifestation. Choose herbs associated with your goal (see pages 102–103) and use them as follows:

- Brew herbal tea and drink it daily until you achieve your goal.
- Blend a lotion and apply it to your skin daily until you achieve your goal.
- Combine essential oils to anoint the symbol of your goal or the parchment on which it is written for the manifesting spell on page 107.
- Burn herbs and resins as incense during the spell.

Herb Pouches

Combine herbs with colour magic by making a suitably coloured origami pouch to store small quantities of dried herbs. You can carry the pouch in a pocket or bag to keep its magical energy close to you.

Manifesting Goddesses
Most manifesting goddesses are related to conception:
- Astarte: conception
- Demeter: conception
- Epona: conception, healthy pregnancy
- Hathor: conception
- Hestia: new home
- Inanna: conception, peace
- Kuan Yin: conception
- Venus: luxury goods, art

Neptune

Manifesting Gods
There is a god for nearly everything you could possibly want to manifest. These are a few of the more popular ones:
- Hermes: holiday, contact with a lost friend
- Jupiter: electronics, material objects, repayment of a debt
- Manannan Mac Lir: good weather
- Mercury: holiday, transportation
- Min: conception
- Neptune: travel by sea
- Tiw: justice

Demeter

Thanking the Deities

After achieving your goal, offer the gods a gift of thanks. Try any of the following:

- Cast the symbol you used into moving water, such as a river or the ocean.

- Sprinkle wine on the ground.

- Sprinkle cornmeal, bread or another offering on the ground.

- Write your thanks on parchment and burn it to transmit your message to the heavens.

- Meditate and thank them during your spirit journey.

Parking Space Charm

When you are driving to a popular destination, you probably expect to spend some time hunting for a parking space. Save yourself the trouble by manifesting the space before you arrive. As you drive, visualize several spaces being open in the parking lot. See yourself pulling into one without waiting. Repeat this charm just before entering the lot:

'O great goddess of beauty and grace, help me find a parking space.'

Basic Manifesting Spell

Adapt this spell for your own specific goal and perform it on the day and hour associated with it (see pages 34–35 and 102–103).

(see pages 34–35 and 102–103)

1 Cast the circle and call the quarters (see page 101). Invite the deity you have chosen to join you. Use words such as: '[Deity], god(dess) of [goal], please join me on this night as I manifest my goal of [goal]. Please lend me your power so that I may receive what I seek.'

(see page 101)

2 Light the candle. Hold the symbol of your goal in both hands and visualize yourself in your new home, your new car, holding your child or enjoying your holiday.

3 Write your full name on the symbol. If it will not fit, write your name, goal and time frame on some parchment. Either wrap the parchment around the symbol or set the symbol on top of it and say: 'Success is mine. My [goal] awaits me. As I will, an' it harm none, so mote it be.'

4 Thank the deity for his or her help. Use words such as: '[Deity], thank you for joining me tonight as I manifested my goal of [goal]. Thank you for your assistance. Stay if you will, go if you must. Farewell and blessed be.'

5 Release the quarters and open the circle. Let the candle burn down. Leave the symbol on the altar until you have achieved your goal. After your goal has manifested, make an offering to the deity who helped you.

You will need:
- Candle in a colour associated with your goal
- Symbol of your goal – for example, travel brochure picture for a holiday, keys for a new car or home, mother-and-baby picture for conception
- Parchment paper (if symbol cannot be written on)
- Pen in associated colour

BANISHING SPELLS

Although Witches do not cast hexes or other harmful spells, there may come a time when you need to banish someone from your life in order to prevent harm from coming to you. Banishing spells can also be used to remove a negative trait or situation from your life. Banishing should not be taken lightly, but it can be very powerful when used properly.

Banishing Goals

Everyone experiences negative thoughts, self-limiting personality traits or difficult situations. Sometimes magic can help to alleviate them. Common reasons for banishing spells include:

- Debts
- Fear
- Broken heart
- Illness
- Self-doubt
- A person interfering with your life
- War
- Natural disaster
- Poverty (personal or global)

Banishing Pentacle

- You can add power to the banishing spell opposite by drawing a banishing pentacle over the parchment with your finger or oil.
- The traditional upright symbol is drawn in one go, starting at the top point down to the lower left point.
- The upside-down banishing symbol begins at the lower left point up to the top point.

Banishing Stones

Black stones, especially onyx and obsidian, help to remove negativity from your life. Smoky quartz and jet are also powerful.

Smoky quartz

Traditional

Banishing

Banishing Herbs

Several herbs are associated with banishing spells:

- Mugwort
- Pepper
- Rosemary
- Sandalwood
- St John's wort

St John's wort

Banishing Negativity

Follow these steps to banish negativity from your life on the new moon.

You will need:
- Black candle
- Rosemary oil or incense
- Athame or wand
- Chalice filled with water
- Parchment paper
- Black pen
- Cauldron

1. Cast the circle and call the quarters (see page 101). Light the candle and incense. Invite the goddess to join you, saying: 'Lady Hecate, guardian of the crossroads, please join me as I seek to remove negativity from my life and embark on a new path.'

2. Point the wand or athame at the chalice. Imagine white light coming down from the goddess and filling the cup and say: 'I charge this water by your spirit to banish the negativity. Let the light fill its place.'

3. Write on the parchment whatever is holding you back from the things you truly want to achieve, such as your anger, fear and frustrations. Hold the paper in your hands and say: 'No more will I be held back by this negativity.' Light the paper from the candle and drop it into the cauldron. As it burns, feel your negativity melting into the earth.

4. Pick up the chalice and say: 'Let light replace the darkness in my life.' Drink the water, imagining white light filling your body as you do so.

5. Release the goddess, saying: 'Thank you Hecate, goddess of the crossroads, for helping me leave the negativity on the old road, as I pass onto the new road. Stay if you will, go if you must. Farewell and blessed be.'

6. Release the quarters and open the circle. Let the candle burn all the way down.

Banishing a Harmful Person

Use this spell to block a person's ability to harm you. If possible, perform the spell on the night of the dark moon, but any night will do in an emergency.

You will need:
- Parchment paper
- Black pen
- Small black canister with a lid (like the kind 35mm photographic film used to come in)
- Small pitcher of water
- Black candle

1. Cast the circle and call the quarters (see page 101). Invite the goddess to join you, saying: 'Hecate, lady of night, goddess of protection, join me and lend me your shield.'

2. Imagine the person who is harming you. Write on the parchment: '[Name], I bind you from bringing me harm. I ask this for the good of all, so mote it be.' Repeat the charm aloud.

3. Put the parchment in the canister, then fill it three-quarters with water. Seal the cap with black candle wax. Hold the canister and imagine peace surrounding you.

4. Release the goddess, saying: 'Lady, thank you for protecting me from harm. Stay if you will, go if you must. Farewell and blessed be.' Release the quarters and open the circle.

5. Put the canister in the very back of your freezer where it will not be disturbed. Let the candle burn all the way down. Once you are confident that the situation is resolved, you can release the spell by opening the canister and letting the contents melt in the sink. Wash away any remaining parchment.

If any large pieces of parchment are still intact after melting the ice, you should either bury or burn them, thanking the goddess for her continued protection.

Lighten the effect
of the spell opposite
by writing on
the parchment:

'[Name], I bind you
from bringing me harm,
but wish you to remain
a positive force in my
life. I ask this for
the good of all. So
mote it be.'

Banishing Colours

Black is the most commonly used colour for banishing spells. However, if you wish to stop someone from harming you without completely severing the relationship (for example, a friend who is unintentionally causing you harm), use a brown candle.

Binding Poppet

If someone has hostile intentions towards you, or is spreading malicious gossip about you, then you are within your rights to stop them. However, an-eye-for-an-eye is not the right approach. Making a binding poppet does not harm the recipient in any way, but it does stop the person from making mischief for you. A binding poppet should only be made if the person is capable of inflicting real harm.

1 Adapt the spell for banishing a harmful person by wrapping black cord around a poppet instead of writing your thoughts on parchment paper. As you do so, repeat: '[Name], you are bound to do me no more harm.'

2 At the end of the spell, take the poppet outside and bury it under a heavy rock. When the person is no longer troublesome, go and retrieve the poppet.

3 Deactivate the poppet by sprinkling it with salt water and saying: 'Your job is done. I take away your name of [person's name] and break the link.' Finally, immerse the doll fully in salt water to cleanse it, then dismantle it and carefully burn the components.

If a person is spreading gossip, you may wish to bind the mouth of the poppet in particular.

LOVE SPELLS

Love spells can be simple or complicated, but if pursued with a pure heart, they are nearly always effective. Traditional love spells and charms have been passed down through millennia, but new spells continue to be created. In addition to spells, folk charms and superstitions can also provide insight into love.

The Time of Love

The hour of Venus on a Friday is the best time for a love spell. Friday is also named after the love goddess Freya. The full or new moon will add oomph to any love spell.

Love Magic Ethics

You cannot force someone to love you, so you should never ask for the heart of a specific person. If you try anyway, you might wind up three times more in love with them than they are with you. You will also never be able to trust that the love is true. Instead, wait until you are ready to find love, but are not interested in a specific person, and then cast a love spell for an ideal mate.

Love Gods
Like their divine female counterparts, most love gods are also associated with fertility:
- Angus Og
- Cupid
- Eros
- Frey
- Shiva
- Tane

Love Goddesses
Love goddesses are found in most cultures. Many are also associated with beauty, sex and fertility.
- Aine
- Alalahe
- Aphrodite
- Astarte
- Freya
- Hera (but do not invoke her if you are not looking for marriage)
- Inanna
- Ishtar
- Isis
- Lakshmi
- Oshun
- Venus

Freya

Spell to Meet Your Perfect Partner

Perform this spell on a Friday when the moon is new, waxing or full.

1. Cast a circle and call the quarters (see page 101). Invite the love goddess of your choice to join you, saying: 'Goddess [Name], please join me on this blessed night. Lend me your energy as I perform this rite. Help me find the mate I desire. Let him [or her] fulfil the qualities I require.' Light the incense and pink candle.

2. Write a list of all the qualities you want in a mate onto the parchment paper with the red pen. Include a time limit for your search (usually 3–6 months). Holding the paper in your hands, feel the satisfaction and joy that the relationship will produce and say: 'Goddess [Name], please guide this person into my life.'

3. Light the parchment in the candle flame, and then drop it into the cauldron to burn away.

4. Release the goddess, saying: 'Goddess [Name], thank you for joining me in my quest, and thank you for bringing me the mate I request. Farewell and blessed be.'

5. Let the candle burn down. Scatter the ashes in a moving body of water or bury them in the garden.

6. Be on the lookout for your new partner. Get out and date. Your partner is out there, but you have to help.

Red creates fiery, short-term love and passionate nights.

Pink symbolizes and creates romantic love.

Dreaming of Your Future Husband

Several old folk traditions feature young women dreaming about their future husbands. In addition to the love charm below, try any of the following:

- Sleep with some wedding cake under your pillow on St Agnes Eve (20 January).
- On Halloween, sit in a dark room lit only by a candle. Gaze into a mirror and eat an apple or comb your hair. Your future husband will appear over your shoulder.
- Peel an apple in one long piece. Swing the peel around your head, and then throw it over your shoulder. It will land in the shape of your future husband's initial.
- Study the palm of your non-dominant hand (the one you do not write with). Look for lines that form an initial on the mound below your ring finger. That will be your future husband's initial.

Love Stones

Use these stones to give your love spells a magical boost or add spark to the bedroom:

- Amber
- Garnet
- Moonstone
- Pink tourmaline
- Rhodochrosite
- Rose quartz
- Ruby
- Watermelon tourmaline

Pink tourmaline

The Scent of Love

Place a piece of amber resin in your bedroom to infuse the room with the scent of love.

Amber

Love Charm

Legend states that you will dream of the person you will marry if you sleep with a mirror under your bed. Try it yourself on the next full moon. First, light a pink candle and put it next to your bed (a birthday candle will do). Gaze into a small mirror and say the charm. Blow out the candle, and place the mirror under your bed (not under your pillow).

'Goddess of the moon, lady of enchanted light, show the face of my beloved to my dreaming sight.'

The Magic of Food

- If you are planning a romantic dinner, consider adding edible flowers to the salad.
- A rosewater risotto is a truly seductive dish. Rosewater can be found in many Middle Eastern speciality shops.
- For a sexy dessert, serve strawberries or cherries over rosewater-infused cake. Drizzle the top with wine-flavoured chocolate sauce.
- Ask a love goddess to bless your meal beforehand, saying: 'Goddess of love, lady of romance, please bless this night with passion and pleasure.' Light candles dressed in love oil (see page 135), rose oil or ylang ylang oil. Place rose petals and a pink quartz heart on the table.

A chocolate and strawberry dessert is perfect for igniting passion.

Use a pink quartz heart to enhance romance.

Calendula

Love Herbs
Herbs and flowers associated with love and passion can be used loose, as cone or stick incense or as essential oils. They include:
- *Rose*
- *Lavender*
- *Ylang ylang*
- *Jasmine*
- *Rosewood*
- *Calendula*

Jasmine

BEAUTY SPELLS

Beauty spells come in two forms – spells to enhance your beauty from the inside out, and spells to enhance your appearance to others without any actual physical alteration. The latter kind are called glamours. If you want to change your appearance permanently, you will have to do the hard work of diet, exercise and hygiene, but these spells can help you to stay motivated.

Beauty Herbs
Herbal beauty products are very popular. Many of the herbs these products incorporate are traditionally used in beauty spells and treatments. The herbs and other natural ingredients most commonly used are:
• Camomile
• Lavender
• Lemon verbena
• Orange blossom
• Rose
• Rosemary
• Witch hazel
• Yarrow
• Honey

Mythological Beauties

The great beauties of mythology and history still colour our beliefs about beauty today. Take heed from the lessons of these myths. Beauty is something to appreciate, but do not let it become an obsession.

Flower of Adonis

• Helen's beauty ignited the battle of Troy.

• Narcissus fell in love with his reflection in a pool of water and died for want of a drink from it.

• Adonis was such a beautiful child that Aphrodite hid him with Persephone, who then refused to give him back.

Mint

• Mint is named after a beautiful nymph who was turned into the plant by Pluto's jealous wife.

Folk Beauty Practices

In addition to love charms, the ancient peoples also had numerous traditions relating to beauty:

- Bathing in the morning dew will enhance your beauty, especially on a Friday morning.
- Cleopatra bathed in milk and honey to keep her skin supple.
- Women bathed in ground rosemary three times a day to ward off wrinkles and old age.
- Washing the face with lady's mantle was believed to maintain beauty.
- Beauty sleep took place during the two hours before midnight, and was worth more than the hours that followed.

Cleopatra

Beauty Glamour

Cast a glamour through simple visualization immediately before you want the effect to take place. Quieten your mind and imagine yourself the way you want to appear to others. In your mind, see your appearance subtly shift. Start small, such as making yourself seem taller or your skin brighter when you are feeling down. Say:

'Beauty bright
and beauty right,
let me be seen
in a new light.'

Beauty Stones
Aside from adorning yourself with gorgeous stones, you can also use them to enhance your beauty spells. Some commonly used stones include:
- Malachite
- Peridot
- Opal

Malachite

Beauty Colours
If a colour looks good on you, then it is appropriate for a beauty spell. However, certain colours are traditionally associated with beauty.

Yellow, the colour of the sun, is connected to beauty.

Use red if you need to reflect the beauty of health and vigour.

Appearance Charm

To boost your confidence in your appearance, stare into a mirror as you repeat this charm three times:

'I am strong, I am pretty, I am bright. All will look upon me with delight.'

Weight-loss Charms

People gain weight for different reasons. For some, it is the result of a slowing metabolism and a less active lifestyle. For others, it is the result of an emotional struggle, either from trauma or low self-esteem. Although weight loss requires exercise and a change of diet, say these three charms whenever necessary to help with motivation:

1 *'I have power over food. Food does not rule me.'*
2 *'My body is a gift and I respect it.'*
3 *'I see the beauty in myself and reflect it to the world.'*

In legend, Aphrodite was born from the sea foam near Aphrodite's Rock in Cyprus.

Beauty Gods

Although most deities related to beauty are female, there are some rather attractive gods who can also be called upon. They are often also associated with youth.
- Adonis
- Angus Og
- Apollo
- Narcissus

Beauty Goddesses

Ancient mythology is filled with goddesses who can still be called upon to grant the gift of beauty. Often, they are also associated with love, fertility and motherhood.
- Aglaia
- Aphrodite
- Arianrhod
- Branwen
- Freya
- Hathor
- Isis
- Lada
- Lakshmi
- Oshun
- Uma
- Venus

Weight-loss Spell

Perform this spell on a new moon during the hour of Venus (see pages 34–35) to help you overcome the emotions that prevent weight loss.

1 Bathe with lavender or rosemary body wash, then go to your ritual space naked. Cast the circle and call the quarters (see page 101).

2 Invoke the goddess, saying: 'Lady Aphrodite, goddess of beauty, icon of the female form, please join me as I seek to recognize the beauty in myself and restore my body and my health.'

3 Stroke the rosemary oil onto the blue candle and then light it. While it burns, list your eating triggers on the first piece of parchment. Hold the paper and say, 'These triggers no longer hold sway over me. Food has no power over me.' Light the paper and put it in the cauldron.

4 Stroke the lavender oil onto the pink candle and then light it. Stare into the mirror and repeat each of the weight-loss charms opposite nine times. Write them onto the second piece of parchment.

5 Thank the goddess, saying: 'Lady Aphrodite, great beauty of the other realm, thank you for sharing your gifts. I treasure them as I treasure my body. Farewell and blessed be.'

6 Release the quarters and open the circle. Place the parchment on the refrigerator door or near your trigger foods. Repeat the three charms into a mirror nine times every night until you reach your goal weight.

You will need:
- Rosemary or lavender body wash
- Rosemary oil
- Lavender oil
- Blue candle
- Pink candle
- Two pieces of parchment paper
- Pen
- Cauldron
- Mirror

Rosemary

HEALING SPELLS

Healing spells can be used for anything, from a broken heart to a physical ailment. They can also be used to resolve a rift between two people or relieve suffering. If you know someone who is very ill, a healing spell is also the only time you can cast a spell on them without their express verbal consent.

Bast

Healing Methods

Many Witches combine one or two healing methods with spellwork to complete the mind–body connection. When appropriate, Western medicine is also recommended. The alternative disciplines most commonly employed are:
• Herbal remedies
• Reiki
• Acupuncture
• Aromatherapy
• Bach flower essences
• Reflexology
• Massage
• Chakra balancing
• Crystal healing

Healing Goddesses

Each culture includes several healing goddesses. You can also call upon a deity associated with the reason for the healing, such as a love goddess to heal a broken heart. The goddesses most commonly called upon are:
• Aine
• Airmid
• Argante
• Bast
• Brighid
• Cerridwen
• Eostre
• Hygeia
• Ganga
• Isis
• Oshun
• Panaceia
• Sulis

Healing Gods

Although the gods of healing are less numerous than goddesses, there are still a few you can call on.
• Apollo
• Asklepios
• Geb
• Horus
• Nuada
• Orunmila

Healing Herbs

Modern medicine began with the healing power of herbs. Although most herbs should be reserved for use by professionals, you can begin your healing with the following herbs made into teas, lotions or added to bathwater:
· Dandelion root
· Echinacea
· Lavender
· Milk thistle
· Nettles
· Rosemary
· Thyme
· Valerian
· Verbena

Milk thistle

Spell to Mend a Broken Heart

Perform this spell on a Friday or Saturday. For other types of emotional wounds, choose Saturday or the day most closely associated with the subject of your pain (for example, Thursday for a job loss; see pages 34–35).

1. Cast the circle and call the quarters (see page 101). Burn the incense.

2. Invite a healing deity to join you. For a broken heart, ask for a love goddess, such as Isis. Say: 'Great goddess Isis, please join me, as I purge my heart of pain. Please release me from this hurt so that I can build a stronger relationship in the future.'

3. Light the black candle. Focus on your pain, and as the feelings consume you, write it all out on the parchment. Light the parchment from the candle and drop it into the cauldron, saying: 'As this parchment burns, so burn my pain and sorrow. I release them to the universe and free myself from the suffering.'

4. Light the white candle. Feel white light descend from the heavens or the moon and fill you with love and peace. Say: 'Lady, I am healed. The pain is gone. The suffering is no more. I am ready to go forth into the world with peace and love.'

5. Release the goddess, saying: 'Great goddess Isis, thank you for joining me and bringing me renewal. My heart is at peace. Farewell and blessed be.'

6. Release the quarters and open the circle. Let both candles burn all the way down.

You will need:
- Rosemary oil or incense
- Black candle
- White candle
- Black pen
- Parchment paper
- Cauldron

Isis

Visualize your heart mending as you work the spell.

How to Heal with Stones

Stones and crystals can be powerful healing tools. You can use them to draw out negative energy or amplify positive energy as part of a wider healing effort. If using a clear crystal, cleanse it when it becomes cloudy (see page 22). For other stones, cleanse them at least once a week during heavy illnesses. These are some of the ways you can use stones to heal:

- Rebalance your chakras by laying on your back and placing an appropriately coloured stone on each chakra point (see page 17).
- Carry a clear quartz with you while healing from an illness or broken bone.
- Place a clear quartz crystal next to your bed while unwell.
- Place an onyx pyramid on your body for 15 minutes to draw out negative emotions.

Camomile tea

Folk Healing Traditions

Folk medicine has survived over the centuries because it can work. Try the following popular folk remedies:

- Drink camomile tea for menstrual cramps.
- Hang wind chimes outside your door to ward off negative spirits.
- Sit in a steam room for any ailment except a heart condition.
- Eat chicken soup for a cold or flu – science has proven that it really does work.

Healing Stones

Nearly every stone possesses healing powers, but the following are frequently found in the Witch's healing toolbox:

- Agate
- Amber
- Carnelian
- Citrine
- Clear quartz
- Copper
- Lapis lazuli
- Onyx
- Red jasper
- Topaz

Agate

Healing Charm

When you are very ill, a full spell may be difficult to perform. Instead, light a blue candle and invoke a healing goddess like Brighid to help you charge a chalice of water with healing energy. Say:

*'I charge this water for healing.
May it purge my body of illness
and restore me to new strength.'*

House Blessing Spell

You should perform this house blessing when you first move into your home. Repeat it on the new moon after a difficult illness or period in your life.

You will need:
- White candle for each room; for safety, stand each candle in a secure holder, on a plate or similar
- Sage wand (see page 137)

1   Light a candle in each room of your home, then return to the entrance. Invite the goddess to join you, saying: 'Lady Hestia, goddess of hearth and home, please join me as I bless my home for peace, love and abundance.'

2   Light the sage wand from the nearest candle. Walk through every room, singing: 'Happy, happy, joy, joy!' Wave smoke around every door, window, vent, plug, tap or pipe where energy can enter or leave your home.

3   As you enter each room, state a blessing for the purpose of the room. For example, sustenance and abundance in the kitchen, laughter and community in the living room, great sex and restful sleep in the bedroom, health and cleansing in the bathroom, or prosperity and wisdom in the office. Use words to the effect of: 'Goddess, bless this bedroom with peaceful sleep and satisfying sex.'

4   Return to the entrance and say: 'Lady Hestia, this house is blessed. I thank you for granting me peace, love and abundance. Stay if you will, go if you must. Farewell and blessed be.'

sage wand

Note: If you have smoke detectors and sensitive neighbours, consider disconnecting them for this ritual only. Reconnect them as soon as you have finished.

FriendShip SpeLls

Our friendships help to define us, but it can be difficult to make new friends once you have left the playground. It can be even more difficult to repair a friendship that has been ruptured by a fight, hurtful words or harmful actions. Whether you want to form new friendships or repair an existing one, these spells will help you do so.

New Friends Charm

Use this charm to help you feel more confident in new situations where you could make friends or win allies. Imagine yourself surrounded by pink light. To win friends in the office, say: 'With confidence and grace, I win allies to my case.' To meet new friends wherever you are, say: 'With confidence and grace, I attract friends in this place.'

Friendship Gods

Friendship is generally considered a feminine attribute, so there are not many gods assigned to this task, but you could look to the gods associated with love, especially Frey. Other options include:
• Airyaman
• Apollo
• Damon
• Iolaus

Hera

Friendship Herbs

Friendship is sweet, and therefore so are many of the herbs and plants associated with it. Consider using:
• Lemon
• Orange
• Vanilla
• Sunflower
• Tonka bean

Friendship Goddesses

The same goddesses who help with love spells can also be used for friendship spells. Consider calling upon:
• Aphrodite
• Artemis (female friendships)
• Freya
• Hera
• Kuan Yin
• Philotes
• Venus

Agate

Friendship Stones

Carry one of these stones in your pocket to encourage new friendships or retain old ones:
• Agate
• Pink tourmaline
• Pink topaz
• Rhodonite
• Rose quartz
• Turquoise

Vanilla pods

Spell to Repair a Friendship

You will need:
- Lavender body wash
- Pure vanilla extract
- Pink candle
- Sunflower or sunflower object
- Parchment paper
- Pink pen

If you and a friend had a fight or drifted apart, cast this spell on a Friday night to help repair the rift. Then call your friend and arrange to meet on a Saturday or Sunday so that you can rekindle your friendship.

1 Take a hot shower with lavender body wash; feel any hurt or anger towards your friend drain away. Dry off, then go to your ritual space naked to symbolize your openness and vulnerability.

2 Cast the circle and call the quarters (see page 101). Stroke the vanilla extract onto the candle and light it. Ask Kuan Yin to join you, saying: 'Lady Kuan Yin, goddess of peaceful partnership, I ask you to join me tonight as I seek to repair my friendship with [Name]. Please help us return to harmony and love.'

3 Remember the happy times you had with your friend. When the love in your heart is full, write down everything you appreciate about your friend. Hold the sunflower while you read the words aloud, then say: 'Lady Kuan Yin, goddess of friendship, please bless this flower with your harmonious energy.' Place the sunflower on the parchment.

4 Thank Kuan Yin for joining you, saying: 'Lady Kuan Yin, goddess of harmony, thank you for helping me to restore my friendship. I am blessed and honoured by your gifts. Stay if you will, go if you must. Farewell and blessed be.'

5 Release the quarters and open the circle. Let the candle burn down. Bring the sunflower to your friend as a peace offering.

Kuan Yin

CAREER SPELLS

Although some Witches do not believe in using magic for personal gain, most recognize that it can be a powerful tool for helping you achieve your goals, especially career goals. Whether you are looking for a promotion or a new job, a career spell can give you the boost you need to find the perfect position. Spells can also help you to overcome obstacles like troublesome work colleagues or combative clients.

Career Stones
The colour orange is associated with careers. Consider carrying one of these stones in your pocket during interviews, challenging meetings or difficult work environments.
- Amethyst: office peace
- Azurite: creativity
- Carnelian: interviews
- Citrine: concentration
- Gold: negotiation
- Honey calcite: mental sharpness
- Orange calcite: interviews

Azurite

Career Gods
Although there are many gods you could call upon, these are a place to start:
- Apollo: the arts
- Asclepios: healing
- Frey: prosperity
- Pan: botany, veterinary
- Haephestus: smithcraft, manual labour
- Hermes/Mercury: travel, sales, communication
- Jupiter: business, management, law

Career Goddesses
Consider calling on these goddesses when casting career spells:
- Athena: the military
- Brighid: handicrafts, writing
- Fortuna: prosperity
- Hecate: protection
- Rosmerta: prosperity

Athena slaying a giant.

Golden cinquefoil

Career Herbs
Try any of the following:
- Cedar: employment
- Cinnamon: employment
- Cinquefoil: money
- Lavender: peace at work
- Nutmeg: luck

Confidence Charm
Say these words in front of the mirror for a quick confidence boost before an important meeting:
'Give me Apollo's charm and Athena's insight, so my confidence will sway all within my sight.'

Spell for a New Job or Promotion

1. Cast the circle and call the quarters (see page 101).
   Light the incense. Invite the deity connected with
   your field of work to join you, saying: 'Lord (Lady)
   [Name], god(dess) of [career field], please join me
   as I seek to enhance my career.'

2. Stroke the oil onto the candle and light it. Write
   the qualities you seek in your new position on the
   parchment and a date by which you wish to start.
   Hold the job symbol in your hand and say: 'I charge
   this symbol to guide me to the right job for me.
   Give me confidence in my dealings with my future
   employer.' Visualize yourself applying, going to
   the interview and then being offered the position.

3. Release the deity, saying: 'Lord (Lady) [Name],
   thank you for assisting me with my career and
   leading me to the right position. Stay if you will,
   go if you must. Farewell and blessed be.'

4. Release the quarters and open the circle. Let the candle burn all
   the way down. Carry the career symbol with you when searching
   for jobs, and for a week into a new job. After you are secure in
   your new job, burn the parchment and offer thanks to the deity.

You will need:
- Cedar incense
- Cedar or cinnamon oil
- Orange candle
- Parchment paper
- Pen
- Symbol of the job, such as a pen for a writing job or a small set of scales for a legal job; use a carnelian crystal if you cannot find a symbol that will fit in your pocket or bag

Protect your position in the workplace by carrying an amethyst crystal or a lavender pouch.

PROSPERITY SPELLS

Prosperity spells are not limited to receiving additional money. It can also involve eliminating debts or creating an atmosphere of positive financial flow in your life. A prosperity spell can help you to achieve nearly any financial goal, except for winning the lottery. If spells could help with that, every Witch would be a millionaire.

Prosperity Symbols

To introduce prosperity into your life, consider decorating your home with some of these prosperity symbols:
- Chinese prosperity dragon
- Ganesha statue
- Gold coins
- Gold box
- Frog figurine
- Lakshmi statue
- Lion figurine
- Money tree
- Pig figurine

Brahma

Prosperity Gods
Most cultures had a god of prosperity of some sort. Many were also related to the fertility of the earth:
- Bel
- Brahma
- Cernunnos
- Frey
- Ganesha
- Jupiter
- Sucellos
- T'shai Shen

Prosperity Herbs
Several herbs are associated with prosperity. They can be used as incense, oil and sometimes tea.
- Allspice
- Cedar
- Cinnamon
- Cinquefoil
- Nutmeg
- Patchouli
- Peppermint
- Sage
- Sassafras

Verbena

Prosperity Goddesses
There are a number of prosperity goddesses who can bring you abundance:
- Abundantia
- Anu
- Epona
- Fortuna
- Habondia
- Lakshmi
- Rosmerta
- Sarasvati

You will need:
- Cinquefoil incense
- Green candle
- Patchouli oil
- Prosperity symbol
- Banknote of any denomination

Prosperity Spell

A Sunday or Thursday is the best day to perform this spell.

1. Cast the circle and call the quarters (see page 101). Light the incense.

2. Invite a goddess and god of prosperity to join you. Say: 'Lady Rosmerta, goddess of abundance and wealth. Lord Cernunnos, god of prosperity and riches. Please join me in this rite of prosperity. Bring me your gifts of wealth and wisdom.'

3. Dress the green candle with patchouli oil, then light it. Hold the prosperity symbol and say: 'I charge this [symbol name] to invite prosperity into my light. This is the guardian of my wealth.' Hold the symbol in both hands and imagine how it will feel to be prosperous, and helping others to benefit as well as yourself.

4. Use the oil to draw a pentacle on the symbol and on the banknote. Place the symbol on the note and say: 'Prosperity is mine. My life is full of abundance and peace. An' it harm none, so mote it be.'

5. Release the deities, saying: 'Lady Rosmerta, Lord Cernunnos, thank you for giving me the gifts of wealth and wisdom. Stay if you will, go if you must. Farewell and blessed be.'

6. Release the quarters and open the circle. Leave the prosperity symbol and banknote in the feng shui prosperity corner of your home (southeast). Let the candle burn all the way down.

Prosperity Stones

Green is frequently associated with prosperity, so green stones are usually helpful, but a few crystals in other colours are also beneficial.

- Amber
- Aventurine
- Emerald
- Citrine
- Green tourmaline
- Jade
- Malachite
- Smoky quartz
- Tree agate

Aventurine

Prosperity and Feng Shui

In feng shui, the southeast corner of your home is the area of wealth and prosperity. Visit this section of your home to see if you have any energy blocks or clutter. Add or remove items as necessary.

- If your bathroom is in this area, close the toilet lid and plug the drains when they are not in use to keep energy from flowing out.
- Avoid keeping rubbish bins here.
- Add a prosperity symbol, such as money or a Chinese dragon, to energize it.
- Add something purple to symbolize wealth.

Chinese prosperity dragon

Purple is the colour of wealth in feng shui.

Gold is associated with money, for obvious reasons.

Green is the colour of growth and abundance.

Debt Charm

Debt holds you back from true prosperity. If you are ready to get out of debt, first make a mental commitment to succeed and then develop a plan. Once your plan is in place, repeat this charm three times each time you make a debt payment. As you say it, see the debt shrink in your mind and feel the peace of being debt-free.

'Debt be gone,
worry be gone.

True prosperity
tomorrow will
dawn.'

Folk Prosperity Traditions

Several prosperity traditions stem from the folk practices of older cultures. You can try a few of these to bring prosperity into your life.

- Carry a carob seed in your purse or bag.
- Plant myrtle or lemon verbena in your garden for long-lasting prosperity.
- Pick up any change that you see on the ground.

Eat lentil soup, especially on New Year's Eve.

Spell for a Raise

If you are happy in your job, but wish you made more money, use this spell before asking for a raise.

You will need:
- Cinquefoil incense
- Peppermint oil
- Green candle
- Silver box
- Parchment paper
- Pen

1 Cast the circle and call the quarters (see page 101). Light the incense.

2 Invite the goddess Fortuna to join you, saying: 'Goddess Fortuna, lady of good fortune and prosperity, I ask you to join me as I seek to improve my fortune and increase the abundance of my salary.'

3 Stroke peppermint oil onto the candle and then light it. Write your goal on the parchment along with the date by which you would like to receive the raise. Visualize yourself being offered the raise, saying, 'Abundance is mine. Good fortune is at hand.' Place the parchment in the silver box.

4 Release Fortuna, saying: 'Goddess Fortuna, lady of good fortune, grantor of prosperity, thank you for joining me as I sought to increase my salary. I am honoured by your gifts. Stay if you will, go if you must. Farewell and blessed be.'

5 Release the quarters and open the circle. Let the candle burn the rest of the way down.

6 Put the silver box near the front centre of your home (when facing inwards from the main entrance). When you receive the raise, burn the parchment and sprinkle wine or bread onto the ground as thanks to Fortuna.

Travel Spells

Although most people enjoy going on holiday,
sometimes travel can be more of a hassle than a
joy. Use these spells to ensure a safe, smooth trip.
Although they will not prevent every delay or
mishap, they will help you to avoid major harm
or complications. Of course, you must also take
appropriate precautions wherever you go – magic
is no substitute for common sense.

Travel Herbs

These herbs are useful in
soothing the common
complaints of travellers:
- Barberry: anti-parasitic
- Camomile: nerves
- Fennel: digestion
- Ginger: nausea
- Ginseng: jet lag
- Peppermint:
  diarrhoea,
  heartburn

Fennel

Travel Gods

There are not many gods
associated with travel,
but these are a few
you might call on:
- Ganesha: general travel
- Hermes: general travel
- Mercury: general travel
- Neptune: sea travel
- Poseidon: sea travel

Goddess of Travel

Athena stands out as one of the few goddesses of travel.
As a woman warrior, she is called upon by solo female
travellers to protect them on their journeys. If you are a
woman travelling alone, change the travel spell opposite
to invoke Athena with these words:

'Goddess Athena,
protectress of
women, join me
on my journey.
Please grant
me your
protection and
guidance, as
I set out alone
to discover
[destination].'

Travel Stones

When travelling, consider
carrying one of these
stones to keep you safe:
- Amber
- Amethyst
- Chiastolite
- Dendritic agate
- Jade
- Kyanite
- Malachite
- Moonstone
  - Yellow jasper

Kyanite

Spell for a Smooth Trip

Cast this spell a few days before you leave. A Wednesday night in the hour of Saturn would be ideal (see pages 34–35).

You will need:
- Purple candle
- Sandalwood incense
- Travel stone
- Piece of comfrey root
- Red pouch
- Parchment paper
- Purple pen

1 Cast the circle and call the quarters (see page 101). Light the candle and incense. Invoke Hermes, saying: 'Lord Hermes, god of travel, please join me on my journey. Please guide the way and help me avoid delays and mishaps. Please grant me a peaceful trip.'

2 Place the stone and comfrey root inside the red pouch. Write your destination, the names of those travelling and the travel charm on the parchment, and then place the parchment in the pouch.

3 Hold the pouch and visualize yourself taking a journey, with no delays and feeling calm and safe.

4 Thank Hermes for joining you, saying: 'Lord Hermes, god of travel, thank you for joining me tonight. Please return to me when I depart and stay with me until my safe return home. Blessed be.'

5 Release the quarters and open the circle. Let the candle burn down. Put the red pouch with your other travel supplies and carry it in your pocket, bag or backpack for the entire trip.

Travel Charm

'This pouch is my talisman. May it protect me on my journey. May it guide me on the safe path, and yet lead me to adventure. May it prevent delays, and yet allow me to linger when I wish. I ask this with harm to none. As I will, so mote it be.'

LOVE POTIONS

Love potions have been around nearly as long as love. From Love Potion #9 to the elixir that put Sleeping Beauty to rest until true love's kiss woke her, we have always believed that magic and love went together. These potions will not have quite the same effect as those mythic brews, but they can help to attract love into your life and then keep it there.

Love Tea

Drink this tea from a pink cup before a date, a romantic evening or casting a love spell. You can also use it to soothe a broken heart. Steep 2 tsp of the blend in 250ml (8 fl oz) of hot water for 5 minutes.

- 2 tbsp crushed rose petals
- 2 tbsp dried lavender buds
- Seeds of 1 vanilla pod or ½ tsp pure vanilla extract

Love Incense

Burn this incense during love spells or to create a romantic atmosphere.

- 2 tbsp crushed dried rose petals
- 2 tbsp dried rosehips
- 2 tbsp dried lavender buds

Passion Incense

Burn this incense when you want to inspire a night of passion.

- 2 tbsp crushed dried rose petals
- 1 tbsp dried jasmine flowers
- 1 tbsp amber resin

Love Lotion

Apply this lotion before a date or a romantic evening with your loved one.

- 250ml (8 fl oz) unscented lotion
- 2 drops rose absolute oil
- 6 drops lavender oil
- 2 drops jasmine oil
- 6 drops ylang ylang oil
- 8 drops rosewood oil

Rosehip flowers

Love Bath Salts

Add 1 tbsp of bath salt blend to the tub before a date, a romantic evening or casting a love spell. You can also soak in it when you need to increase your love for yourself.

Salt and oil blend:

- 3 tsp Epsom salts
- 1 drop rose absolute oil
- 2 drops lavender oil
- 2 drops ylang ylang oil
- 2 drops rosewood oil

Salt and herb blend:

- 3 tsp Epsom salts
- ½ tsp crushed dried rose petals
- ½ tsp dried lavender buds
- ½ tsp dried jasmine flowers

Rose

Love Pillow

Use this small pillow if you want to dream of your lover, or simply to improve the romantic atmosphere of your bedroom.

1 On a Friday night in the hour of Venus (see pages 34–35), place the squares of fabric right sides together and sew along three sides. Turn right side out and stuff with the flower mixture and resin. Stitch the fourth side closed.

2 Hold the pillow in both hands. As you feel it warm between your hands, say: 'Each night I lay down my head, bring thoughts of love to this bed.'

3 Place the pillow under your sleeping pillow or inside your pillowcase. If the scent is too strong, put it under the mattress or under the bed (but make sure that your pets do not make a toy out of it). When the scent starts to fade, refresh it with a drop of love oil, rose oil or lavender oil.

You will need:
- Two 7.5cm (3in) squares of red or pink fabric
- Matching thread
- Mixture of dried flowers and petals, including rose, rosehip, lavender and jasmine
- Amber resin

Use a ready-made pouch if you do not wish to sew.

Love Oil

Apply this oil to a pink candle that you will burn during a romantic evening or love spell, or add it to an aromatherapy lamp to fill your home with the scent of love (and a dash of passion).
- 30ml (1 fl oz) almond or jojoba oil
- 1 drop rose absolute oil
- 2 drops lavender oil
- 1 drop jasmine oil
- 2 drops ylang ylang oil
- 2 drops rosewood oil

Love Body Wash

Use this before any romantic occasion, or to help you learn to love yourself again after a broken heart.
- 250ml (8 fl oz) unscented body wash
- 2 drops rose absolute oil
- 2 drops jasmine oil
- 3 drops rosewood oil
- 1 drop rosemary oil

Carry a little paper pouch of dried petals with you on a date.

HEALING POTIONS

Healing potions are not magical elixirs that Witches bubble and boil in the cauldron. Instead, they tend to be teas, lotions, bath salts, oil blends and incense blends that you can use in spells, drink to soothe your nerves or apply to your skin to enhance your other healing efforts. Substitute the oil blends for the oils suggested in previous spells, or make up your own spells to incorporate them.

Healing Body Wash

A shower is best when healing or banishing negativity, because your negative energy can wash immediately down the drain. If you take a bath, you will stew in the energy for a while. Blend these ingredients to make a body wash. If possible, use a blue bath puff or flannel with it.

- 250ml (8 fl oz) unscented body wash
- 4 drops rosemary oil
- 2 drops lavender oil
- 2 drops sandalwood oil

Soothing Bath Salts

When you are completely stressed out or physically exhausted, use bath salts to soothe both body and mind. Each blend makes one bath.

Salt and oil blend:
- 3 tsp Epsom salts
- 2 drops lemongrass oil
- 2 drops peppermint oil
- 2 drops camomile oil

Salt and herb blend:
- 3 tsp Epsom salt
- ½ tsp lemongrass
- ½ tsp eucalyptus
- ½ tsp camomile

Lemongrass

Relaxation Tea

Drink this tea from a blue cup before bed to help you sleep, or before a difficult event to help you stay calm. Steep 3 tsp of the blend in 250ml (8 fl oz) of hot water for 5 minutes.

- 6 tbsp dried camomile
- 3 tbsp dried lemon verbena
- 3 tbsp dried passionflower

Calming Lotion

If you are angry, irritated or just at your wits end, use this lotion to calm your nerves.

- 250ml (8 fl oz) unscented body lotion
- 6 drops camomile oil
- 6 drops lavender oil
- 4 drops vanilla oil

Invigorating Lotion

Use this lotion if you are run down and need an energy boost.

- 250ml (8 fl oz) unscented body lotion
- 10 drops orange oil
- 2 drops peppermint oil
- 6 drops lemongrass oil

Sage Wand

A sage wand is not technically a potion, but it is made from herbs. In addition to sage, you can make bundles of lavender, cedar or any other non-hallucinogenic and non-toxic herb.

1. Bundle the herbs together with the stems even at the bottom. Starting at the base, wrap the string tightly around the wand. Stop 2.5cm (1in) from the top, then loop back down to the base and tie off. The herbs will shrink as they dry, which will make the wand looser. Tie the wand as compactly as possible to encourage even smoking.

2. Trim the top flat or leave it ragged, and then hang the bundle up for two weeks to dry out.

3. When it is ready, simply light the end. Let the top 1cm (½in) burn, then blow it out so that it continues to smoulder.

You will need:
- Enough long stalks of sage to make a 2.5cm (1in) thick bundle
- Cotton string or yarn (avoid synthetic materials or toxic dyes)

Two sage wands

Cleansing Oil

Burn this oil in an aromatherapy lamp if your space is filled with negative energy and saging is not appropriate. You can also apply it to your temples for a quick emotional cleansing.
- 30ml (1 fl oz) almond or jojoba oil
- 3 drops rosemary oil
- 2 drops thyme oil
- 1 drop lemongrass oil

Relaxation Oil

Relaxation oil can be burned in an aromatherapy lamp, applied to the forehead or added to a bath.
- 30ml (1 fl oz) almond or jojoba oil
- 3 drops lemon balm
- 3 drops lavender oil
- 3 drops passionflower oil
- 1 drop rose or rosewood oil

Putting your oil blends into a suitably coloured bottle will enhance them with colour magic.

CONFIDENCE AND CAREER POTIONS

A high level of confidence goes a long way towards improving your career or any other aspect of your life. At the same time, having a successful career improves your confidence. Use these potions to enhance your career prospects, and improve your confidence and self-esteem so that you can be successful at anything you do.

Confidence Tea
Drink this tea from a yellow cup whenever you need to feel more confident in yourself, your abilities or your appearance. It is especially helpful after an event that bruises your confidence, like a break-up, job loss or bad review. Steep 2 tsp of the blend in 250ml (8 fl oz) of hot water for 5 minutes.
• 2 tbsp dried orange peel
• 1 tbsp dried lemongrass
• 1 tsp dried lavender buds
• ½ tsp dried camomile

Confidence Oil

Use this oil as part of a confidence spell, apply it to a yellow candle to burn before an important event or add it to an aromatherapy lamp whenever your confidence wanes.
• 30ml (1 fl oz) almond or jojoba oil
• 3 drops orange oil
• 2 drops lemon verbena oil
• 2 drops lavender oil

Career Oil

Substitute this oil for other oils called for in career spells, apply it to an orange candle that you burn before an interview or review, or add it to an aromatherapy lamp in your office before an important negotiation.
• 30ml (1 fl oz) almond or jojoba oil
• 3 drops cedar oil
• 2 drops cinnamon oil
• 1 drop nutmeg oil

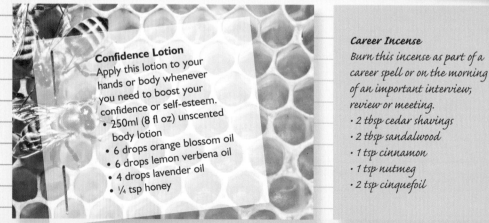

Confidence Lotion
Apply this lotion to your hands or body whenever you need to boost your confidence or self-esteem.
• 250ml (8 fl oz) unscented body lotion
• 6 drops orange blossom oil
• 6 drops lemon verbena oil
• 4 drops lavender oil
• ¼ tsp honey

Career Incense
Burn this incense as part of a career spell or on the morning of an important interview, review or meeting.
• 2 tbsp cedar shavings
• 2 tbsp sandalwood
• 1 tsp cinnamon
• 1 tsp nutmeg
• 2 tsp cinquefoil

Career Pouch

If you are looking for a new job, make a career pouch. Place it in the career corner of your home (north) if you follow feng shui, or carry it with you. If the scent is strong, however, do not take it into the interview with you.

1. On a Sunday in the hour of Jupiter or a Thursday in the hour of the sun (see pages 34–35), lay out all the ingredients in front of you. Calm your mind and picture the type of job you want to attract. On the parchment, write 'I am a [job title]. I earn [salary]. As I will, so mote it be.'

2. Place everything except the pen into the pouch. Hold the pouch and imagine the satisfaction of a job you love and can succeed at. Repeat the words you wrote on the parchment aloud.

3. Once you have the job you want, remove the carnelian from the pouch and then burn the other contents.

You will need:
- Yellow or orange fabric pouch
- Carnelian stone
- Parchment paper
- Pen
- Herb and spice mixture, such as cinnamon, nutmeg, cedar shavings and dried cinquefoil

Make a note of which mixtures are the most successful for you.

Confidence Bath Salts

Soak in these bath salts whenever you are feeling low and need a confidence boost. You can also use it to improve your confidence before an important meeting or event.

Salt and oil blend:
- 3 tsp Epsom salts
- 2 drops lavender oil
- 2 drops orange blossom oil
- 2 drops lemongrass oil

Salt and herb blend:
- 3 tsp Epsom salts
- ½ tsp dried orange peel
- ½ tsp dried lavender buds
- ½ tsp dried lemongrass

PROSPERITY POTIONS

Prosperity potions should be used in conjunction with other efforts to reduce debts or improve your fortunes. None of the potions will help you to win the lottery or magically make money appear in your bank account. They will, however, surround you with prosperous energy that will invite good fortune into your life.

Prosperity Tea

Drink this tea from a gold or green cup before asking for a raise, negotiating a contract or applying for a loan. Steep 2 tsp of the blend in 250ml (8 fl oz) of hot water for 5 minutes.

- 2 tbsp dried orange peel
- I tbsp dried lemon balm
- ½ tsp cinnamon
- I tsp whole cloves
- ½ tsp nutmeg
- ½ tsp dried valerian

Prosperity Lotion

Apply this lotion to the skin before asking for a raise, applying for a loan or negotiating a contract. You can also wear it whenever you need to attract prosperity into your life. Before applying it all over your body, test it on the back of your hand.

- 250ml (8 fl oz) unscented lotion
- 2 drops cinnamon oil
- 14 drops orange oil
- 6 drops cinquefoil oil

sassafras

Quick Money Fix Incense

Burn this incense during spells for an urgent financial need, while completing a loan application or calling someone to ask for money.

- 1 tsp sassafras
- ½ tsp cinnamon
- ½ tsp nutmeg

Prosperity Incense

Use this incense in general prosperity spells, or burn it anytime you need to boost your prosperous energy.

- I tsp frankincense
- ½ tsp cinquefoil
- ½ tsp patchouli
- ½ tsp nutmeg

Prosperity Pouch

Make a prosperity pouch on a Sunday in the hour of Jupiter, or on a Thursday in the hour of the sun (see pages 34–35).

1 Lay all the materials before you. Quieten your mind and imagine a steady stream of prosperity flowing towards you. Place everything in the pouch and pull it shut.

2 Hold the pouch in both hands and say: 'I bless this pouch to bring me prosperity and wealth. So mote it be.'

3 Hang it over the front door to bless your home with prosperous energy and extend that blessing to you each time you depart.

You will need:
- Horseshoe charm or pendant
- Green or gold fabric pouch
- Mixture of dried herbs, including cinnamon, allspice, nutmeg, cloves, cinquefoil, sassafras and orange peel

Prosperity Oil

Use this oil in any general prosperity spell. You can also add it to an aromatherapy lamp to attract prosperous energy into your life.
- 30ml (1 fl oz) almond or jojoba oil
- 4 drops patchouli oil
- 5 drops cedar oil
- 1 drop cinquefoil oil

Quick Money Fix Oil

Use this oil when you need a quick money fix. You can spray it around your office or home, apply it to a green candle before burning or add it to an aromatherapy lamp.
- 30ml (1 fl oz) almond or jojoba oil (for a lamp or candle) or 60ml (2 fl oz) distilled water (for a spray)
- 5 drops cinquefoil oil
- 5 drops cedar oil
- 2 drops cinnamon oil

Debt Oil

If you are trying to pay off debts, add this oil to an aromatherapy lamp or apply it to a green candle to burn while you pay bills. You can also spray it on the bills themselves.
- 30ml (1 fl oz) almond or jojoba oil (for a lamp or candle) or 60ml (2 fl oz) distilled water (for a spray)
- 5 drops sassafras oil
- 5 drops cinquefoil oil
- 2 drops patchouli oil

Index

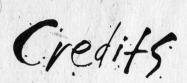

Credits

Key: *a* above; *b* below; *l* left; *r* right; *c* centre

Images used under license from Shutterstock, Inc: Larisa Loftskaya *1 & 2–3 (paper background)*; Melinda Fawver *2 & 74cr (feather)*; Ints Vikmanis *2 & 75cr (key)*; Nattika *2, 73bl & 109 (burnt parchment)*; Ajay Shrivastava *2 & 53bl (Durga)*; injun *2 & 89bl (crystal ball)*; saim nadir *3 (parchment)*; Miguel Angel Salinas Salinas *3 (cauldron)*; Galoff *4–5, 102–103, 125 & 126–128 (paper background)*; Martine Oger *5ar*; Tara Urbach *5 & 98br (wand)*; Kudryashka *6ar*; Igor Dutina *7ar, 96b, 119br*; Yusaku Takeda *9c (book)*; martin garnham *10bl*; alphacell *11bc*; R Gino Santa Maria *12ar*; Saniphoto *13ar*; il67 *14–15 (background), 96–97 (paisley pattern)*; godrick *14b, 22bl*; Roman Sigaev *15, 55 & 97 (parchments), 80r (papers)*; sima *16a*; Wagner Christian *16b*; Austra *17l*; VaclavHroch *18al*; Elena Schweitzer *18ac*; Olivier Vanbiervliet *18ar*; Carmen Sorvillo *18bl, 18br, 19bl, 65br*; Linda *18bc, 20bl, 20bc, 20br, 21bc, 21br, 105ar*; Pakhnyushcha *19al*; iDesign *19ac*; Douglas Freer *19ar*; Elnur *19bc*; TableMountain *19br*; Subbotina Anna *20al, 115br*; Vinnikava Viktoryia *20ac*; max blain *20ar*; Studio Araminta *21al, 139a*; Mefodey *21ac*; Dole *21ar, 136bl*; Martin Novak *21bl*; hoskari *22al, 115cr*; Morozova Tatyana (Manamana) *22a, 23bl, 108ar, 114ar, 117cr, 126a, 132bl*; Alexandar Iotzov *22br, 129b*; nagib *23al*; radarreklama *23ar*; Falk Kienas *23br*; Nic Neish *24, 56a, 64a*; Alice *25bl*; Colour *25ar*; Noah Strycker *26a*; Genevieve Dietrich *26cl*; Rey Kamensky *26br*; Bobby Deal *27ar*; Elena Itsenko *27cl (petals)*; Liv friis-larsen *27bc*; Stephen Coburn *28–29 (sun)*; Torian *28–31 (planets), 36b*; Vladimir Zivkovic *32al*; Mark R *32ar*; Alena Ozerova *32br*; giangrande alessia *33a*; Carolina K Smith, MD *33b*; Fribus Ekaterina *34, 124br*; ilpavone2004 *36a*; Torian *36b*; Jurgen Ziewe *37*; Catmando *38*; Michael Onisiforou *39*; Katarzyna Malecka *40a*; Jurand *40b*; Sergey Prygov *42c (Njord)*; Marek Slusarczyk *42c (landscape)*; James M Phelps, Jr *43b (landscape)*; JIS *44cl, 45ar*; Hano Uzeirbegovic *45cl*; Graca Victoria *45ar (photo corners)*; djslavic *46 (Venus)*; Maksym Dragunov *47c (Neptune)*; David Hernandez *47b*; John Lock *48–49a*; willy12 *48–49b*; Lucian Coman *51al*; michael ledray *51ac*; bouzou *51br*; oblong1 *52a*; paul prescott *52b, 53br*; Rohit Seth *53a*; commodore *54–55 (background)*; CLM *54b, 74cl*; Richard Griffin *60l, 88a*; Hannu Liivaar *60br*; Nataliya Peregudova *61b*; Chris Tennant *61a*; alexsol *62bl*; Mike Flippo *62ar*; Phase4Photography *64cl, 71ar*; Dion van Huyssteen *64br*; Andreas68 *64bl, 65a*; Nicholas Peter Gavin *66cl*; Maciej Sobczak *67br*; Jenny Horne *68l,71cr*; Kirsty Pargeter *71br*; design56 *74a*;

Ioana Drutu *74b*; José *75al*; Alfredo Schaufelberger *76b*; Khirman Vladimir *77l*; argus *77r (yin/yang symbol)*; s74 *78al*; Simon Krzic *78ar*; Reddogs *80l*; Ecoasis *80r (book)*; Darla Hallmark *81a*; M Dykstra *88c*; Duasbaew Alisher *88b*; hektor2 *89a*; Galushko Sergey *89br*; Jovan Nikolic *91a*; Dorner *96–97 (side swirls)*; marilyn barbone *99bl*; Olegusk *99bc*; titelio *99br*; Dmitry Rukhlenko *100c, 100b*; Seana *103ac*; Luciano Mortula *103ar*; Gizele *104*; Georgios Kollidas *106al*; Jose Elias da Silva Neto *106ac*; Filip Fuxa *106ar*; Yellowj *106bl*; Cecilia Lim H M *107ar*; smie *107cr*; LianeM *108br*; Peter Polak *109br*; tobe_dw *111a*; vicko *112l*; Karol Kozlowski *114br*; Lorraine Kourafas *115a*; angelo gilardelli *116b*; Kurilina Tatyana Andreevna *116cr*; Kharidehal Abhirama Ashwin *117a*; Nicholas Georgiou *118c (landscape)*; Zara's Gallery – Click here! *119l (silhouette)*; issalina *120al*; mypokcik *120ar*; Lezh *120b*; Roman Barelko *121br*; Jiri Vaclavek *122c*; Alena Yar *122b*; Sally Scott *123b, 127r (sachet), 137r*; BORTEL Pavel *124bl*; iofoto *125br*; Sergey Chushkin *126bl*; Mirka Moksha *127l*; Aaron Amat *127r (fabric)*; Tamara Kulikova *128b*; James Steidl *129a*; Keo *130a*; Magdalena Kucova *130b*; Johanna Goodyear *131a*; Transition *131b*; letty17 *132a, 134cr*; fafoutis *132br*; Elena Elisseeva *133, 139b*; vera bogaerts *134bl*; matka_Wariatka *136br*; Greywind *137l*; Ronen *138a*; Tischenko Irina *138b*; South12th Photography *140ac*; Kati Molin *140ar*; Alexander Sysolyatin *140b*; Natalia Siverina *141a*; Peter Hansen *141bl*; Jill Battaglia *141br*.

General images: Fotocrisis, Darryl Sleath & Ewa Walicka *(chalice stains on paper)*; David Franklin & kd2 *(polaroid frames)*; samantha grandy *(masking tape)*; mysontuna *(ink splats)*.

All other illustrations and photographs are the copyright of Quarto Publishing plc. While every effort has been made to credit contributors, Quarto would like to apologize should there have been any omissions or errors – and would be pleased to make the appropriate correction for future editions of the book.